NOW HERE COME I ...

seventeen humorous verse plays

by Simon Lavington.

ISBN: 978-1-8381396-0-5

Published by Running Backstays
www.runningbackstays.co.uk

Printed and bound by Ipswich Design and Print.

Illustrations and front cover by Rosalind Lavington

Contents

Introduction.

Different social or educational contexts call for different performances. To give an idea of the flavour of the seventeen plays in this book, we first list the cast and length of each. All the plays have a humorous touch; many of the historical ones contain interesting insights. Some of the pieces are close to being fast-moving slap-stick; five include a little singing. None is trivial.

The cast-lists vary from six to ten actors, with some of the plays making provision for optional extras such as soldiers. Texts vary between 990 words and 3,750 words. To estimate running times, we find that the shortest play (990 words) has a run-time of between about eight and twelve minutes depending on the quantity of elaborate props and the actors' tastes for dramatic embellishment. The longest play could take up to about 45 minutes if the cast really chose to go to town.

The seventeen plays are presented in three groups: eleven scenes from British history; five Shakespeare shortened and one traditional folk tale. In summary:

Short title	***Length, words***	***Number in cast***
A1: Olive Cromwell: a restoration comedy	1,010	7
A2: The Glorious Revolution	1,270	8
A3: The Great Garter	1,340	6
A4: Death of Cardinal Wolsey	1,300	6
A5: Hundred Years War, Part One	2,440	8 + soldiers
A6: Richard Coeur de Lion	2,480	7
A7: Good Queen Bess	2,100	6
A8: The Belle of Naples	3,750	6 + sailors
A9: Eleanor of Aquitaine	2,360	7 + soldiers
A10: The Duke of Bridgewater's Canal	1,100	5 + citizens
A11: Captain Francis Light	1,420	6
B1: Macbeth	1,850	9 + highland chiefs
B2: The Tempest	2,640	10 + waves
B3: Omlet	2,210	8
B4: Midsummer revels	3,120	6
B5: Romeo and Juliet	3,640	9 + soldiers
C1: Suffolk Mummers' Play	990	6

Introduction

The plays are written in verse – usually iambic pentameters. We find these easy to speak. Audiences quickly become attuned to the plot being revealed in manageable couplets. The couplet format also clarifies the cues between actors. In the simpler plays, each character enters with a line beginning "*Now here come I, ...*", rather in the style of many traditional Miracle plays or Mummers' plays. This device reduces the need for elaborate costumes and speeds up the narrative. It also makes classroom reading easier.

The seventeen plays, together with a companion volume containing twelve shorter ones for younger actors, have been written over a forty-year period. All 29 plays have been road-tested by friends and family during many years of merry parties. Our usual habit is to distribute the scripts at the party, participants being aware that there will be no rehearsals. Part of the pre-performance fun is the scramble to the dressing-up box to find vaguely-appropriate props and costumes.

Of course, others may choose to use these scripts in schools or for public performances. One summer, two of the historical plays were enacted by the Grundisburgh Dramatic Society for an open-air Village Fete. A good time was had by all.

The full text of the seventeen plays follows. Finally, background notes for each play are given at the end of the book.

A1. Olive Cromwell: a restoration comedy.

Cast, in order of appearance

Sir Peter Lely,	a portrait painter
King Charles I	
Ms Olive Cromwell	
Prince Rupert	
Thomasina Fairfax,	Cromwell's general
Nell Gwynne,	in an advanced state of pregnancy
King Charles II	

This is no beauty contest!

Olive Cromwell

Scene: the Palace of Westminster in about 1640. The audience may imagine that they are the Members of Parliament. Enter Sir Peter Lely.

Lely: Now here come I, the famous Peter Lely.
It's up to Westminster I travel daily.

For I'm a portrait painter to the rich
And Westminster's a profitable pitch.

I take commissions from the parliament,
And every week I paint a different gent.

(Lely sets up his easel. King Charles enters slowly and pompously).

Today I have a special job to do -
A privilege vouchsafed to very few:

The King himself commands me to this place
To paint a picture of the royal face.

K.Ch I: Now here come I, the great King Charles the First.
You doubt my greatness and you'll come off worst!

Through *God* I am the boss around this place
And here, to symbolise my power: my mace!

(King Charles I places mace on table).

This parliament is here to do my will.
And when I need some cash, it foots the bill.

Come, Lely, paint me in this striking pose,
And show my well-turned leg and regal nose!

(King poses pompously. Lely begins to paint. Enter Olive).

Olive: Now here come I: my name is Cromwell, Olive.
I say this scene is all pretence and folly!

The King proclaims he rules by God's decree;
His Parliament would tend to disagree.

It is to *Parliament* that power belongs,
And we intend to right the royal wrongs.

K. Ch.I: Who is this woman? What is this she says?
She preaches contrary to nature's ways!

It's natural that all be ruled by Kings.
Why can't a woman understand these things?

Olive: The rights of men and women do equate!
I say: 'Omnipotence is out of date!'

Your majesty: the Good Book is our guide.
Pray, do not try to swim against the tide.

(Olive holds up a copy of Germaine Greer's book The Female Eunuch. Enter Prince Rupert).

Pr. Rupert Now here come I, Pwince Woopert, woyal champ.
Upon this female wubbish will I stamp!

A King's a King, and ever more shall be.
Come, waise the woyal flag and follow me!

(Rupert raises a banner, on which is written 'Kings rule OK'. Enter Thomasina).

Thom. F: I'm Thomasina Fairfax, Olive's mate.
We women think that Olive's simply great!

A Parliament'ry standard we shall raise,
So, shed your shackles! Follow *women's* ways!

(Thomasina raises a banner, on which is written 'Iron thighs rule OK').

Olive: The men around this place are hard to bear.
Their attitude is far too cavalier!

Lely: I hardly think that *I'm* a cavalier –
Of battles I intend to keep well clear.

Yon monstrous regiment of iron thighs
Makes opposition seem a bit unwise.

(Lely makes as if to hide).

K.Ch.I: Come, Rupert: let us men defend the right;
These hags will run as soon as there's a fight!

Olive: The rights of every woman is our goal.
We'll fight for this, whatever be the toll!

(A fight commences. The women get the upper hand. Lely peeps out, as King Charles and Rupert exit, beaten).

Lely: I see the King and Rupert lose the day –
So for this portrait I will get no pay.

I'd better change the subject of my pic.
Instead of Charles, I'll try and paint that chick.

Olive: How *dare* you call me 'chick'! Don't use such words!
We'll show you men that we're no flock of birds!

Come, Fairfax, let's reorganise this place.
Remove that bauble which they call the Mace!

(The mace is removed).

We puritans need no adornment now.
There's no man here to whom we need to bow!

Lely: Ms Cromwell, may you have the best of health!

(Lely bows humbly to Olive).

And, now that you protect our Commonwealth,

Perhaps you'd care to have your portrait done?
Your picture could be quite a lot of fun.

Olive: Oh, paint away! But mark! I'll pay you nought
Unless you paint me plain, with every wart!

(Olive adopts a glowering pose. Lely begins to paint).

Thom.F: Oh Olive! I've conceived a super plan:
A Parliament without a single man!

Let every woman join our sacred cause:
A new beginning, and an end to wars ... (whores?)

(Enter Nell Gwynne)

Nell G: Now here come I, the beautiful Nell Gwynne;
Not innocent, and not exactly slim!

Your politics I do not understand,
But may I join your liberating band?

Olive: Since you're a woman, you are welcome here,
And we'll protect your int'rests, never fear.

Nell G: Well, can I bring along another pal,
A friend I met whilst walking down the Mall?

Olive: Why, yes! *All* friends of yours are welcome here.
We women count our friendships very dear.

(Nell beckons. Enter King Charles II).

K.C.II: Now here come I, King Charlie number two.

Olive: Another King? What *am* I going to do?

This is the end! I cannot break my word.
Farewell, cruel world! .... I'll fall upon my sword!

(Olive dies extravagantly).

K.C.II: Oh dear! That's not a very pretty sight!
D'you think I gave the dame a sudden fright?

I only came along to be with Nell.

(Charles II turns to Fairfax).

I hope you don't shove off your coil as well!

Thom.F: My coil's all right, so let us all relax,
And cease from making rods to beat our backs.

This feminism's too extreme by half,
So let us all be *humans* for a laugh.

K.C.II: Sweet Nell and I can recommend the part.
We've got this mutual loving to an art!

Nell: A merry monarch, scandalous and poor –

(Nell points wryly at Charles II).

But better than a tyrant or a bore.

(Nell points doubtfully at the body of Olive)

Lely: Well, *I'll* be poor if I don't sell this pic.
Some restoration here will do the trick.

(Lely begins to paint. Charles and Nell embrace. Fairfax admires the painting and/or Lely.)

A man, a woman: Charles and Nelly meet.
At last my human picture is complete!

End.

A2. The Glorious Revolution, *or Brother James's Heir.*

Cast, in order of appearance:

Samuel Pepys	a civil servant, the narrator for our play
King James II	son of Charles I and brother of Charles II
Princess Mary	James II's elder daughter by his first wife
Queen Mary of Modena	James II's second wife, an Italian
Princess Anne	James II's younger daughter
Sir Christopher Wren	represents informed Whig opinion
Sir Isaac Newton	also represents informed Whig opinion
Prince William of Orange	husband to Mary.

Well, that was quite easy!

Glorious Revolution

The action takes place in London, between 1685 and 1689. Enter Samuel Pepys.

Pepys: Now here come I, my name is Samuel Pepys.
Although few know it, I'm the one who keeps

A secret diary. Here's the very book!
It's full of intrigue. Come, let's take a look:

It's 1685 - a fateful year
With changes for the worse, as you shall hear.

Our merry monarch, scandalous and poor,
Has died. Alas, King Charlie is no more.

(Enter King James)

James: Now here come I, I'm Charles's brother James –
(We Stuarts do have *such* confusing names!)

Pepys: King James the Second! Welcome to the throne –
(And may you have the sense your brother's shown).

James: There'll be some changes now that I am King.
The Parliament's too strong. Another thing:

I'm Cath' lic, and I therefore cannot stand
The Church of England's hold upon this land.

All power in the kingdom should be mine.
I hereby claim it as of Right Divine!

(Enter Mary)

Mary: Now here come I, King James's daughter, Mary.
My father's rantings make me very weary.

Oh Daddy! Give the Protestants a chance,
And don't take so intolerant a stance!

James: Begone, you milk- sop maid! Get out of here!
If only I'd a sturdy *son* as heir!

Pepys: If James's second wife produced a son,
Then Parliament's reforms could be undone.

Mary: Don't talk of babes! My step-mum whom I hate
Is ever these days in a pregnant state.

I'm off to Holland: I can stand no more.
I'll visit Bill, the cousin I adore.

(Mary exits)

James: Good riddance! Now to stiffen up this realm,
The State shall feel a *Cath'lic* at the helm!

(Enter Queen Mary).

Queen: Now 'ere come I, ze King's Italian vife.
I've suffered James' ardour half my life!

As you can see, once more I am with child.
Zis passion for a boy: it makes me wild!

Pepys: The King's two daughters, Protestants the pair,
Would be displaced if *she* produced an heir.

(Enter Anne)

Anne: Now here come I, the other daughter, Anne.
My sister Mary's safely with her man.

But I must stay and help my step-mama,
Before the King's excesses go too far.

Come on, old dear, you'd better take a rest –
That's quite a bulge you have beneath your vest!

(Anne & Queen exit. Enter Wren).

Wren: Now here come I, Sir Christopher W-ren.
I wepwesent the English Gentlemen.

I am an architect of some wenown.
Perhaps you've seen my plans for London town?

I am a Whig; no Tory toad am I.
For Parliament alone I'll live and die!

Your majesty, the people are afwaid
Of all the changes you have lately made.

You cancel laws that Parliament has passed,
Your awogance leaves Ministers aghast.

James: How dare you, Sir! I'll follow ev'ry chance
To make the State of England more like ... France.

Pepys: Though France is England's oldest enemy,
King Louis is a friend of James, you see.

(Enter Isaac Newton).

Newton: Hello! Sir Isaac Newton is my name.
My scientific work has world-wide fame.

I study Apples at the Varsity,
And write reports of utmost gravity.

I come with news of serious unrest
Concerning the *Indulgence* and the *Test*:

Your Majesty, the clergy cannot heed
The Declaration they were told to read.

The seven bishops who contest your power
Now find themselves imprisoned in the Tower.

And worse: the Universities complain
That you have shut a College down again!

James: Enough! I have no time for wingeing wets.
The Army waits at Hounslow to the West.

I shall dissolve the Parliament today.
I'll call the troops if Members disobey!

Wren: Come, good Sir Isaac – this has got to stop!
The King's gone mad! He's heading for the chop.

Newton: We need a plan. Perhaps the milk-sop maid
And Orange Bill will rally to our aid?

(Enter Anne and the Queen, clutching her stomach).

Anne: Quick, Quick! You men! The Queen's about to pod.
Stop scheming, and start praying to your God.

Pepys: Now here's the moment we've been waiting for.
If it's a boy, we're doomed for evermore!

Queen: It's coming! Gather round! What pain! What joy!
There's no pretending: it's a little boy!

(Queen holds up a bundle – which might be a baby boy)

Anne: It looks pretend to me! It's far too slender.
I think its name should be the Old Pretender!

Pepys: The Jacobite Pretender he'll be called.
He'll keep the hopeful Cath-o-lics enthralled.

James: At last! A Cath'lic son! Let's thank the Lord!
The Stuart dynasty is now assured.

Anne: King Louis and the Pope may well be glad,
But I and all my friends are really sad.

(Anne goes to Pepys to be comforted. The Queen goes to James II to be comforted).

Pepys: Your sister Mary's married to the man
Who'll help us all, if anybody can.

Newton: Prince Will-i-am of Orange is his name.
He lives in Holland, where he's quite a flame.

Wren: A splendid chap! He's Protestant, he's strong,
He hates the French and so we *can't* go wrong!

Glorious Revolution

Newton: I've sent the message. Bill is on his way.
They say his troops arrive here any day!

James: What's that you say? Prince William coming here?
To take the throne will cost him very dear!

Anne: Oh, please don't fight! You might get hurt! You know
The English troop's morale is very low.

Newton: The country won't support you in the row.
You've bullied us enough, so give up now.

James: Oh, what am I to do? Should I not fight?
This throne is mine alone by Heav'n-sent right!

Newton: I hear Prince William's landed at Torbay!
They say the people shouted out Hurray!

Queen: Ve'd better cut and run. Zis is no time
To sit around debating Right Divine.

James: Oh well, I see I've sadly lost my chance.
Let's go and take a holiday in France.

(James and Queen exit).

Pepys: There goes a King who courted too much piety,
And tried to turn the clock back on Society.

(Enter William and Mary).

William: Now here we come: it's Will-i-am and Mary
To help restore you from events contrary.

I see this Throne is vacant. What's the game?
To leave it getting cold would be a shame.

Newton: Hoy! Not so fast! Before you take a seat
There's several conditions you must meet.

We have a Bill of Rights that you must sign,
The Parliament'ry power to enshrine.

(Pepys presents some paperwork for William to sign).

And here's another Act of Toleration
Which gives religious freedom to this nation.

William: All right, I'll sign. It means a quiet life
For Royal Willie and his darling wife.

(William sits on the throne. Mary sits on his knee; they embrace).

Wren: So ev'rything has now turned out alwight:
A Wevolution – and without a fight!

(Wren and Newton exit).

Pepys: Let Parliament assume the power instead.
We've played our part, my dear, and so to bed!

(Pepys and Anne walk off arm in arm, leaving William and Mary cuddling).

End.

A3. The Great Garter.

Cast, in order of appearance

Jocelin of Brakelond,	an old Bendictine monk at St. Edmund's Abbey, Suffolk.
Stephanie Langton,	putative Archbishop of Canterbury; in dispute with the King.
Roger Bigod,	Earl of Suffolk and Norfolk,
Black Shuk,	the Earl's fierce dog.
Queen Isabella	of Angoulême, wife of King John.
King John of England:	

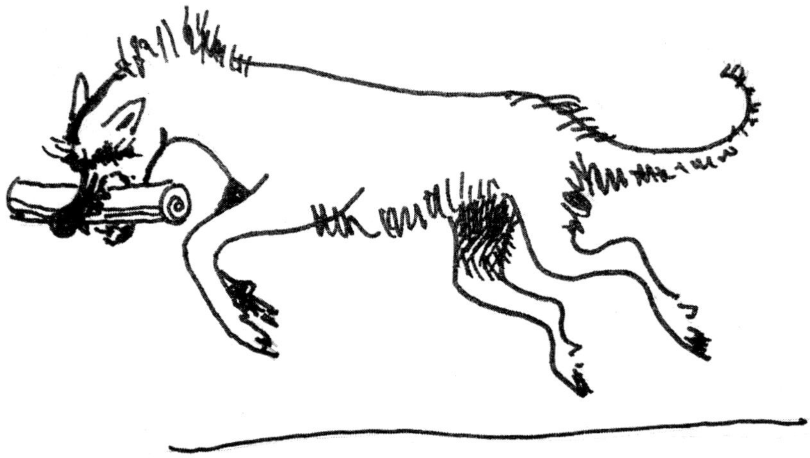

I would have preferred a peasant.

The time is November, 1214. The action takes place first of all in the Abbey at Bury St. Edmunds, then at Runnymede (near Windsor) the following June.

Act 1: the guest house at St. Edmund's Abbey, in front of a log fire.

(Enter Jocelin).

Joc.: Now here come I, old Jocelin's my name.
I have a deal of trouble to explain.

A Benedictine monk for 40 years,
I've had my fill of monasterial cares.

The reason why these clothes are rather shabby
Is that we're deep in debt at Bury Abbey.

St. Edmund's Abbey's famed throughout the land,
But our affairs are getting out of hand.

(Enter Stephanie Langton).

Stef.: Now here come I, the Rev'rend Stephanie.
I've come from France to visit my new See.

Joc.: Why, Steffie Langton! Welcome to this place!
With all this gloom, it's good to see your face.

We've heard that you're in trouble with the King.
Come by the fire, and tell us everything.

Stef.: Well, as you know, it is the clergy's wish
That I become the very next Archbish.

The Pope in Rome approved their choice of me
To fill the job at Canterbury's See.

But our King John's against my ordination.
He thinks of it as women's liberation.

And 'liberal' is one thing that he's not.
He says that justice is a load of rot!

Joc.: He's set aside our Liberty of Bury.
Illegally he's taxed us with a levy.

And though we've had the Abbot's due election,
He's now refused to sanction our selection!

King John has no respect for us poor folk!
The way he acts has gone beyond a joke.

Stef.: Unless we act to curb this tyrant's power,
The outlook for this land is pretty dour.

(Enter Earl Roger Bigod).

Rog.: Now here come I, I'm Roger Bigod, Earl.
Down on your knees, young Stephanie my girl!

There's none in Suffolk that don't bow the knee
To mighty Roger Bigod, Earl – that's me!

Its cold in here! More warmth is my desire.
Black Shuk! Come, put a peasant on the fire!

(Enter Black Shuk, the dog, with a log in his mouth).

B.S.: Now here come I, Black Shuk, Earl Roger's dog.
I couldn't find a serf, so here's a log.

Whatever I'm commanded, I obey.
I serve the Earl, my master, night and day.

Rog. What's this I hear? King John been making trouble?
High time we burst that monarch's pompous bubble!

He really is a bit incompetent –
He lost a battle on the continent.

He tried to confiscate my fav'rite castle!
We barons shouldn't stand such blatant hassle.

Stef.: I don't care if he's good or bad at war.
My main complaint is that he breaks the law.

His father, Henry Second, ruled us well;
But King John's reign is turning into hell!

We really need to keep these kings in hand –
Some kind of common *Charte*r for this land?

Rog.: I don't know what a Charter's all about.
I think he needs a smack upon the snout!

B.S.: My snout's been smacked until its black and blue.
I'd rather have a Charter, wouldn't you?

Rog.: Be quiet, you cur! The time has come for force.
A hearty thrash will make him change his course.

I'll tell the other barons of my plan:
I know they will support us to a man.

From what I've heard of them, I have a hunch
They'd like to give the King a Suffolk Punch!

(Earl Roger exits).

Steff.: Black Shuk, your master is a fearsome fellow.
He thinks a Charter's pacifist and yellow.

But, once King John has signed this Bill of mine,
All English Kings will have to fall in line.

B.S.: Let's go and keep the hot-head in control.
I'll help you to achieve your Charter goal.

(Steff. & BS exit).

Joc.: What luck! the barons and the clergy too!
A combination that's a powerful brew!

I feel that Steffie's Charter cannot fail,
And that our Abbot soon will drink his ale.

For, once the King is bridled with their fetter,
Affairs at Bury Abbey must get better.

I'd better go and help them find the King,
And see the climax of this Charter thing.

(Jocelin exits).

End of Act 1.

Act 2: a meadow by the River Thames at Runnymede, seven months later.

(Enter Queen Isabella).

Isa.: Now here come I, the fair Queen Isabelle –
A trifle woe-begone, as you can tell.

King John, my husband, lacks a certain charm,
So I've escaped here for a spot of calm.

He's always forcing me to kiss and cuddle,
Which leaves my lovely hair all in a muddle!

This place called Runnymede looks good for resting –
Safe for a moment from the King's molesting.

(Enter King John).

King: Now here come I, King John: you've heard of me!
I'm King of England and of Normandy!

Why, here's me wife! .... What, hiding from your lord?!
Give us a kiss, you luscious little broad!

Isa.: Remove your hands, you thoughtless, dirty creep!
Your rudeness is enough to make me weep.

And, anyway, your ign'rance is a bore:
The French took Normandy in 1204.

King: Go back to France, you garlic-eating wench!
If *I* can't kiss you, go back to the French!

(Enter Roger with drawn sword, followed closely by Steffie, Black Shuk and Jocelin. Steffie bears the Charter (Magna Carta)).

Rog.: Enough of that! Your game has got to stop,
Or in your mouth this trusty sword I'll pop!

King: Good grief! I think he means it! This is treason!
Your boldness, Sir, had better have good reason!

Joc.: We've come to ask you to obey the law,
And stop oppressing people, rich or poor.

King: Well, sod the Law! I can do anything!
Dieu et mon droit. By God, I am the King!

Steff.: The barons and the clergy all demand
That you must sign this Charter in my hand.

King: What is this foolish bit of tatty paper?
Clear off, you lot, and stop this monstrous caper!

Rog.: Up with your rantings we'll no longer put!
Until you sign, I'll not withdraw a foot!

You've got to yield and, by St. Edmund, Martyr,
I'll make you listen while we read our Charter.

(They begin to read from the Charter).

Steff: "No punishment without a proper trial;
A law that's free from prejudice or guile."

Rog.: "Preserve our ancient rights and Liberties,
Which were, of course, created for our ease."

Joc.: "No overlord must persecute his vassal;
All English yeomen should be free from hassle".

B.S.: And, finally, accept the ordination
Of Steffie here, the darling of the Nation!

King: Oh, very well, I'll sign the wretched thing,
But please remember that I'm still the King.

By signing, I have stopped a revolution
And started up the British Constitution.

Isa.: Three cheers for us! I feel a new-born girl.
Thanks for your help, you strong and handsome Earl!

Rog.: In Framlingham I have a mighty castle;
Come up and see me for a spot of wassail!

B.S.: I think we need to fasten up this Charter.
Can Steffie help by lending us her garter?

Steff.: For you, Black Shuk, I'll gladly show a leg.
You've helped us, so there is no need to beg.

(Steffie removes her garter & wraps up the Charter).

Joc.: Our Charter's signed and sealed, as is our play.
So let us celebrate this fateful day!

End

Great Garter

A4. The Death of Cardinal Wolsey *or Alas, Poor Tom.*

Characters, in order of appearance.

Thomas Wolsey	Cardinal, Chancellor of England.
King Henry VIII	(complete with cod-piece)
Anne Boleyn	highly fancied by Henry.
Catherine of Aragon	Queen, when the play opens.
Mistress Lark	a Suffolk bar-maid & close friend of Wolsey's.
William Goldwin	schoolmaster of Wolsey's College at Ipswich.

Who are you calling fat?

Act 1: at the Royal Court, London, about 1525.

(Enter Thomas Wolsey).

Tom: Now here come I, Tom Wolsey is the name.
I'm sure you're all familiar with my fame.

I started small: an Ipswich butcher's son;
But now to wealth and eminence I've come.

As Chancellor of England I have *power*!
I make all men - except the sov'reign - cower.

As Cardinal, I'm told there's every hope
That one fine day they'll even make me Pope!

(Enter Henry VIII).

Henry: Now here come I, King Henry number Eight.
That Cardinal I really start to hate!

He disregards the nobles and the landed.
He thinks he runs the country single-handed!

He may be good at raising tithes and tax,
But as a priest he's really rather lax.

He has his hand in everybody's purse -
And keeps a fortune for himself, what's worse!

(Enter Anne Boleyn).

Anne: Now here come I, the nubile Anne Boleyn.
I am his Grace the Duke of Norfolk's kin!

In high society I've got my niche -
Unlike fat Wolsey, who is nouveau riche.

For many months the King's made eyes at me,
And lately we've been cuddling secretly.

And, now I've had a sample of his charms,
I long for him to take me in his arms!

(Anne embraces Henry and his cod piece. Enter Catherine of Aragon).

Cath.: Hands off that piece! You don't know where it's been!
And anyway, its *mine*, for I'm the Queen.

My name is Cath'rine Aragon, you see.
I won't let Henry make a fool of me.

For I'm the lawful wife of Good King Hal,
So that's hard luck for any other girl!

Come, Wolsey, can't you tell the King to stop
His fooling, and give Anne Boleyn the Chop?

Wols.: I'll do my best; I've never liked her sort.
Her flirting brings disgrace upon this Court.

Anne: You hypocrite! You have your wenches too!
For we all know the naughty things you do!

Although as Cardinal you've never wed,
There's many-a Suffolk girl who's warmed your bed!

Cath.: How dare you mock a Cardinal of Rome!
You should be kept in check, and sent back home.

Anne: Oh, you and Wolsey! You are both the same.
You fear for what they'll think in Rome or Spain.

I'm off! And, Harry, if you love me true,
Get rid of Wolsey - else I'll not love you.

(Anne exits).

Cath.: Well, that's the end of her, for none would dare
To sack Tom Wolsey, that is crystal clear.

Henry: I'm King round here, and I sack who I choose!
And as for Rome, I've nothing there to lose.

I've had enough of you! Go to your room!
I loathe your tired and unproductive womb!

Cardinal Wolsey

(Catherine exits in tears).

Towards Queen Cath'rine I feel no remorse.
I must dispatch her with a quick divorce.

Hey, Wolsey! Write a letter to the Pope,
And say my marriage hasn't any hope.

Get a divorce, and get it pretty quick,
For Cath'rine's coldness makes me really sick.

I'm off to spend a long weekend with Anne,
For she can do the things that please a man!

(Henry exits).

Wols.: I fear that Anne has turned our sov'reign's head.
I'm sure he wants to get her into bed.

He is obsessed with siring many-a son,
And Cath'rine hasn't born him even one.

I cannot fix divorce: the Pope won't play.
Perhaps young Anne will cool if I delay.

I'll not disturb the European scene
Simply because a King dislikes a Queen.

Besides, I've other projects to advance -
Like balancing the powers of Spain and France.

(Wolsey exits, shuffling state papers).

Act 2: the same place, some months later.

(Enter Mistress Lark).

Lark: Now here come I, a humble Suffolk maid.
My name is Mistress Lark, and I'm afraid.

I've never been to London town before,
And how I reached this Court I'm not quite sure.

But I must find a certain Cardinal
And tell him that he's not behaving well.

For Wolsey had his wicked way with me,
Then promised that we'd marry rapidly.

But off he went and left me all alone.
So now I've come to turn his heart of stone.

(Enter Goldwin).

Gold.: Now here come I, Bill Goldwin is the name,
A Suffolk schoolmaster of no mean fame.

I'm noted for my diligence and knowledge;
I'm Head of Wolsey's brand new Ipswich College.

But lately I've been feeling less than jolly:
I fear the school is running out of lolly.

I've come to plead with Wolsey for some cash
Because his College dream's about to crash.

It seems we both have bus'ness with my Lord.
Let's hope he's here at Court, and not abroad.

(Enter Wolsey, shabbily-dressed and looking worried).

Wols.: It's me again, though who'd believe my story?
I am a shadow of my former glory.

Gold.: My Lord the Cardinal? Can it be you?
Whatever's happened? What on earth's to do?

Why are you dressed in rags, and why alone?
Have all your chaplains and your servants gone?

Lark: Alas, my Lord: you don't look very well.
Have you been robbed and beaten? What befell?

Wols.: No common thief or ruffian did this thing.
The man who fixed my downfall was the King!

He saw I would not get him a divorce
And so he bullied me without remorse.

He took away my titles and my land -
I've nothing but the clothes in which I stand.

Lark: Alas, poor Tom! You're down to my estate.
Come home with me and be my own true mate.

Wols.: I fear I cannot. Here's the awful reason:
The King will shortly have me tried for Treason.

Whate'er the verdict, I'm as good as dead.
I'll rot in gaol, or lose my head instead.

In fact, I feel too ill to face a trial.
If I must die, ... then let me die .... in style!

(Wolsey dies dramatically and elaborately).

Lark: He's surely dead! ... So now I'm all alone.
Good Master Bill: please, can you take me home?

Gold.: All right. Come home and be the College matron.
Let's try to run the place without our patron.

I see the Pride of Ipswich sinking fast.
Without Tom's help, the College may not last.

Lark: I've heard Queen Cath'rine was his friend at Court.
Why don't you try and ask for her support?

(Catherine enters in a hurry, pausing only to say):

Cath.: No good: I'm disillusioned with this land.
You English rats! I won't give you a hand.

(Catherine exits haughtily).

Gold.: Perhaps our hope now lies with Anne Boleyn?
For after all, she has got Suffolk kin.

Cardinal Wolsey

(Anne enters in a hurry, pausing only to say):

Anne: Sorrree! .... I'm disillusioned with the King.
He's fat and rude, and only wants one thing!

(Anne exits, pouting).

Lark: Perhaps the King can find a good solution,
And cheer us up from all this disillusion.

(Henry enters in a hurry, pausing only to say):

Henry: Dissolve the monast'ries, and grab their stash!
Now that's a good idea! I'm strapped for cash.

I'll start with Suffolk. Bury Abbey's loaded.
It's time the Abbot's treasure was eroded.

(Henry exits, rubbing his hands).

Gold.: If Tom were with us, he'd have drawn the line.
He'd not have let them spoil St. Edmund's Shrine.

This marks the end of Suffolk's years of ease.
These nouveau Tudors! They do what they please!

Lark: St. Edmund and our Tom have had their day.
On this sad note we end our little play.

(Mistress Lark and William Goldwin embrace and remain with heads lowered).

End

A5. The Hundred Years War, Part One.

Cast, in order of appearance for Act 1:

The Ghost of the Black Prince	who lived from 1330 - 1376.
Baldrick,	an English peasant.
Mistress Quickly,	a London bar-maid.
The Duke of Burgundy,	a French nobleman.
Sir Edmund,	an English nobleman.
Henry V	began to reign in 1413, aged 26.

Cast, in order of appearance for Act 2:

The Dauphin,	son of King Charles VI of France.
The Duke of Burgundy,	
Henry V	
Baldrick,	now equipped as an archer.
'Bob'	Mistress Quickly as a boy archer.
The Ghost of the Black Prince.	

The Dauphin could be played by Sir Edmund, if short-staffed. Several young people could make up the French army in Act 2.

One day I'll get the hang of this

Act 1: London in 1413.

(Enter the Ghost)

Ghost: Now here come I, a ghost! King Edward's son!
I'm called the Black Prince, so in black I come!

I died too young to wear the English crown,
But old enough to gain a knight's renown.

We fought the French at Poitiers, and won.
We even took the French King captive home.

We ransomed him for huge amounts of gold --
And ev'ry soldier got a share, I'm told.

But that was all of 50 years ago
And since those glorious days, there's naught but woe.

Abroad, the French King's confidence has grown.
The peasants started to revolt at home.

(Enter Baldrick)

Baldrick: Now here come I, a peasant through and through.
I'm Baldrick the Revolting. Who are you?

Ghost: I led your yeoman fathers in the fray:
We fought at Crecy and at Poitiers.

You English archers brought us victory
Against the French - our ancient enemy!

Baldrick: Well, that was long ago. I've done with wars.
War never brought good harvest or just laws.

I'd rather stay at home and drink and dance
Than fight to keep your roy'l estates in France.

(Enter Mistress Quickly)

Quickly: Now here come I, men call me Mistress Quickly.
I'm quick to give a bit of slap and tickly!

Old Baldrick boasts of liking dance and drink:
He's good for nothing else, I rather think.

I wish Prince Hal was here: now *there's* a man
To stand up to the French, if any can!

(Enter Duke of Burgundy)

Burgundy: Now here come I, le Duc de Burgundy.
I'm on a mission of diplomacy.

I'm looking for King Henry and his court.
A message from the Dauphin have I brought.

(Catches sight of Mistress Quickly, & starts to kiss her hand)

Bonjour, Ma'mselle! I kiss your pretty ring!
Please tell me where I'll find your English King.

Baldrick: Hey, Frenchy! What's your game? Put that girl down!
We don't want foreigners in London town!

Quickly: Hands off! Forget your continental manners!
The King comes soon. Look, see the royal banners.

(Enter Sir Edmund with pomp & ceremony, followed by King Henry)

Edmund: Now here come I, Sir Edmund, with my sword.
Make way for our most noble sov'reign lord!

Ghost: About time too! The English badly need
A King who's just, ... and strong,... and fit to lead!

(Ghost exits quietly, smiling).

Henry: Now here come I, King Henry number Five.
I'm 26 years old, with lots of drive.

I used to be 'Prince Hal, the good-time guy',

(Blows a kiss at Mistress Q., who blows one back).

But now for nobler things I mean to try.

My Great Gran'dad, King Edward number Three,
Owned half of France in 1363.

Through female line, he claimed the Frenchies' throne –
A claim I hereby take up as my own!

Burgundy: Folie de grandeur! What a load of merde!
We Frenchmen think your claim is very wierd.

Your old estates in France are all in tatters;
We've taken back the land that *really* matters.

The Dauphin sends a message in this sack.
He says your English claim's a load of cack!

(Hands the sack to Henry)

He'll challenge you to combat in the field
He says he'll thrash your army till you yield.

(Henry opens the sack, which contains tennis balls. Henry examines them in disgust)

Henry: A load of balls? What sort of gift is here?
The Dauphin's insult sure will cost him dear!

Sir Edmund: throw away this childish packet.
We'll give the Dauphin's balls a thumping racket!

Edmund: Begone, foul Frog! Go back and tell your Master
That soon he'll face defeat and great disaster.

(Burgundy exits, looking apprehensive).
(Edmund addresses Baldrick).

The Dauphin's nothing but a jumped-up brat.
He's not allowed to treat our King like that!

Come, Baldrick: now's the time to raise an army.
We must invade. To dally would be barmy.

Baldrick: Our cause is just: I know you must be right,
But, as for me, I'd hesitate to fight.

You've got your suit of armour, 'cos you're wealthy.
I haven't got a helmet --- most unhealthy!

Quickly: Well, *I* would fight for Hal, our Handsome King.
In fact, for Hal I'd do most anything!

Baldrick: All right, I'll fight, although it might be hell;
And, Mistress Quickly, why not come as well?

You're fit and strong. I have a cunning plan.
When we reach France we'll dress you as a man.

Henry: A good idea! We'll call you 'Private Bob' --
And in short trousers you'll look just the job!

I'll give you both fair wages, and the chance
To make some cash from ransoms, when in France.

We'll land in Normandy, and march to Arras,
And then we'll turn sharp right and capture Paris!

So come, brave hearts, we're ready to advance.
Let's not delay: fair stands the wind for France!

(All exit)

Act 2: France.

(Enter the Dauphin)

Dauphin: Now here come I, the Dauphin: quite a beau --
The toast of all of Paris, don't you know!

King Charles the Sixth of France is my old Dad.
However, nowadays he's gone quite mad.

So I command the army in his stead --
There's forty thousand men, and me their Head!

Our enemies will find I'm just the chap
To knock them sideways with my *Force de Frappe*!

The English army landed weeks ago
I don't expect they'll cause us bother, though.

(Enter Burgundy)

Burgundy: It's me again, the Duc de Burgundy,
With news of English gains in Normandy.

They've captured Harfleur. Now they march North-West.
Let's intercept them. Which location's best?

Dauphin: They're tired and hungry. Let them march some more.
We'll meet them near a place called Agincourt.

At Agincourt I plan to set a trap.
The English force will fall into our lap!

(Dauphin and Burgundy exit, smiling conspiratorially. After a short delay, enter Henry, followed closely by Baldrick and 'Bob' (ie Mistress Quickly dressed as a boy in short pants)).

Henry: Well done, you men! We must keep marching on,
Although I know you're feeling none too strong.

Press on! Don't let those Frenchies wear you down.
We've covered 60 miles since Harfleur town.

Bob: The siege of Harfleur: that was touch and go --
For plague and sickness proved the greater foe.

From dysent'ry did many fellows die.
"Once more into our breeches" was the cry.

Baldrick: Sir Edmund's dead; the Earl of Suffolk too --
We seem to be a much-depleted crew.

This wet October weather gets my goat.
I'm cold and hungry, and I've lost my coat.

Bob: Why don't the French attack? We're nearly done.
Their men outnumber us by five to one.

Henry: Keep moving, chaps! If we can reach Calais
The English garrison will save the day.

(All three march in line round the stage once or twice, and then exit. After a suitable pause, all three march on stage again, but this time looking very weary and dispirited).

Bob: We've marched another day -- I don't know how.
We're very tired. Oh, Hal: where are we now?

Henry: We're somewhere near a place called Agincourt.
It's safe to rest. Our feet are very sore.

(They form a little huddle, taking up a position where they will eventually bed down for the night).

Now, Baldrick: go and use your scouting skill.
Perhaps the French are camped behind that hill.

(Baldrick exits purposefully. Once Baldrick has gone, 'Bob' and Henry become very close)

Bob: Oh, Hal! I fear we're all about to die.
The thought of battle makes me want to cry.

Henry: Don't worry, Bob, our men will never waver.
They know the English longbow is their saviour.

Our archers shoot their arrows with such force
They'll stop a knight in armour -- and his horse!

(Baldrick re-enters, Henry & Bob stop embracing)

Our bowmen are the best: of that, no doubt!
Come, Baldrick, tell us: what have you found out?

Baldrick: Behind that hill are hoards of well-armed French.
I found them by their awful garlic stench.

There must be forty thousand men, or more.
Tomorrow they'll attack us, that's for sure.

Henry: It's getting dark. Let's sleep; we all need rest.
Don't worry, men. I know you'll do your best.

(Darkness falls. All three huddle down on the ground in a tight group. Hal comforts Bob).

And gentlemen in England now abed
Are lucky that you're fighting in their stead.

Baldrick: We few, we very few, we band of brothers
Could wish that we were safely with our mothers.

Bob: Tomorrow morning is St. Crispin's Day
So to St. Crispin we had better pray.

(They all fall silent. It is night. After a suitable pause, the French (ie the Dauphin and the Duke of Burgundy & soldiers) creep on stage and stand silently and menacingly to one side. To simulate a great army, some children hide inside a large duvet cover, on which is painted the silhouette of many soldiers. The English do not notice the French. There is a pregnant pause. The lights come up, as dawn breaks).

Baldrick: Ah, dawn at last! Is everybody well?
I didn't sleep: that awful garlic smell!

Bob: The King looked after me, so I'm all right --
A little touch of Harry in the night!

(Blows a kiss at Henry, who blows one back)

Henry: I wonder where the French are? ... …

(Turns round and sees the French for the first time)

.. .. Bloody Hell!!
The place is stiff with Frenchies, armed as well!

(The three English hastily get to their feet and form a line of battle facing the French. Bob and Baldrick get their bows ready at the front, and Henry brandishes his sword behind them).

Dauphin: Just look at those pathetic English bows!
They wouldn't be much use for scaring crows!

Those archers look like under-nourished midgets!
Let's have some fun: let's amputate their digits.

(Makes rude continental one-fingered gesture)

Baldrick: Here's two strong fingers that you'll never sever,
And they shall draw my bow-string tight as ever!

(Makes a two-fingered English rude gesture at the French)

Bob: We few, we happy few, we band of brothers.
We'll make the French run crying to their mothers!

Burgundy: We'll rid the continent of England's menace.
Cry, "Vive la France, the Dauphin, and St. Dennis!"

Henry: We'll prove our mettle in the battle's forge.
Cry "God for Harry, England, and St. George!"

Dauphin: My knights in armour: Charge the English line!
You'll soon break through and vict'ry will be mine!

(Burgundy and his silhouette of soldiers lunge forward)

Baldrick: Come on, you Frogs! I'll easily shoot you dead!
Your armour can't resist my arrow-head.

(Burgundy falls down and the duvet cover collapses round him. After a brief pause, he crawls back to the French lines, quickly re-erects the duvet cover, and simulates another company of soldiers).

Dauphin: Charge them again! They can't resist for long,
For they are weak and we are fit and strong.

(Burgundy charges again, in company with the duvet- covered children).

Bob: You may be strong, you're also rather slow.
You cannot dodge the arrows from my bow.

(Bob shoots Burgundy, and the duvet cover collapses. After a pause, Burgundy crawls back to the French lines, quickly re-erects the duvet cover, and pretends to be yet another company of soldiers).

Dauphin: Mon Dieu! This battles' progress is unpleasant!
Our noble French are shot at by a peasant!

So, charge again, and never mind the hits.
Just let me see those English cut to bits.

(Burgundy charges again with the duvet cover. He dies again. This time, he remains in a crumpled heap, as does the duvet).

Henry: Well done, my archers! Give the French what-for!
We've killed ten thousand; are there any more?

Dauphin: I yield! I yield! Our losses are too great.
I won't have *any* army at this rate.

(Kneels beneath Henry's sword).

Henry: Do you accept my right to claim your throne?
Will you restore the lands I rightly own?

Dauphin: When Daddy dies, you shall be king of France.
Meanwhile, your French estates I will enhance.

(Dauphin stands up)

I'll go and give our mad King Charles his cue --
His daughter Cath'rine has her eye on you!

(Dauphin exits)

Baldrick: Thank goodness! Now this bloody battle's over,
I'll seize some booty and return to Dover.

(Drags off the bundled duvet with Burgundy, and exits).

Bob: There's little place for Mistress Quickly here,
For Hal has plans for marriage, so I fear.

(Bob looks down-cast, and begins to wander listlessly off).

Henry: I'll travel home with you across the water,
Although I want the King of France's daughter.

(Hal puts a comforting arm round Bob. They begin to exit, but then Hal turns round, pauses, and says reflectively:)

Let Englishmen take note: we won! And hence
In future show two fingers to the French!

(Enter Ghost)

Ghost: Hey, not so fast! I've sombre news for you.
The French recover in the War, Part Two.

They find a secret weapon, Joan of Arc,
At Orleans she really makes her mark.

(Hal and Bob turn and exit, Hal gesticulating in disbelief)

So now our little play has nearly ended,
And in its course was Hist'ry slightly bended.

At least we did without those Tudor leeks,
And in their place presented Bob's fair cheeks!

So -- raise a cheer to end our little play:
To Bob and Baldrick: Archers saved the day!

(Loud cheering is heard off-stage. Ghost bows and exits.

From off-stage, the cheering turns into the theme music from The Archers --- Da di Da di Da di Da, Da di Da di Daaah Daaah etc.)

End.

A6: Richard Coeur de Lion *or Franks Incensed.*

Cast, in order of appearance.

Richard I	King of England, aka Coeur de Lion, Lionheart.
Philip	King of France.
Eleanor	of Aquitaine, Queen Mum, Richard's mother.
Saladin	Sultan of Syria & Egypt; head of Saracen army
Guy de Lusignan,	titular King of Jerusalem, later of Cyprus.
Blondel	faithful minstrel to King Richard.
Berengaria,	Princess of Navarre; married Richard in Cyprus.

Enough!

Richard Coeur de Lion

There are six Acts:
Act 1: Vezeley, France, July 1190.
Act 2: Acre, Palestine, April 1191.
Act 3: Cyprus, May 1191.
Act 4: Acre, June 1191.
Act 5: Germany, spring 1193.
Act 6: London, March 1194.

Act 1. In France, near Vezeley; July 1190.

(Enter Richard)

Richard: Now here come I, King Richard, Lionheart,
And in this play I take the major part.

I'm King of England, and I have in hand
A vast array of continental land.

The greater part of France belongs to me:
From Cherbourg to the Medit'ranean sea.

(Enter Philip)

Philip: Now here come I, King Philip, Roi de France.
I'll stop your boasting! Vous êtes fol, je pense!

There's trois divisions over which you reign:
Anjou and Normandy and Aquitaine.

But all the rest of France belongs to moi!
So, be respectful, else it's au revoir!

(Enter Eleanor)

Eleanor: Now here come I, Queen Eleanor, Queen Mum.
Young Richard is my very fav'rite son.

In time, I hope he'll conquer more of France.
Against him, Philip doesn't stand a chance.

(Tums to harangue Richard).

You ought to marry and produce a son.
Without an heir, our dynasty's undone.

I've just the girl for you. She's from Navarre;
A princess known as Berengaria.

Richard: Oh, Mother! Do leave off your marriage-broking.
Besides, I love my minstrel … … only joking!

(Eleanor and Philip look horrified for a moment)

Eleanor: Behave yourself! I order you to wed!
Your bride will come and meet you in the Med.

For you two lads should go on a Crusade.
The Franks in Palestine require your aid.

The Muslim Saracens are growing stronger.
The Franks can't hold the Holy Land much longer.

Philip: The Saracens have got a mighty chief
Called Saladin: his strength's beyond belief.

Crusading can be quite a dang'rous thing;
I'd rather stay at home and just be King.

Richard: Brace up, old man! It is your Christian duty
To go out East. Besides, there's lots of booty!

I'd rather like to meet this Saladin.
I'll march right up and biff him on the chin!

Philip: *Eh bien!* I'll give the Eastern Franks a hand.
I'll cross the Alps and travel overland.

(Philip exits).

Richard: That's fine. I'll travel out another way.
I'll go by sea, departing from Marseilles.

(Richard exits).

Eleanor: Farewell! All Christendom relies on you.
Jerusalem has fallen, Acre too.

Though, privately, I think it's all a shame.
Crusading, frankly, is a messy game.

(Eleanor exits. End of Act 1).

Act 2: The Frankish crusader camp at the siege of Acre, April 1191.

(The scene opens with Saladin looking up over the castle walls which form the Acre fortifications).

Saladin: Now here I am, the Sultan Saladin,
And this is Acre that you see me in.

My town of Acre's very strongly fenced
By thick stone walls, which makes the Franks incensed!

For eighteen months they've camped around the town.
They bash these walls, but fail to knock them down.

But hark! Some Frankish soldiers come this way.
I'll hide and listen in to what they say.

(Saladin crouches down behind the castle wall. Enter Guy.)

Guy: Now here come I, I'm Guy of Lusignan.
I've summoned help from ev'ry Christian man.

I ruled Jerusalem. Then, what a rout!
The Saracens came round and threw me out!

So now I'm fighting back as a Crusader.
And here we are today, besieging Acre.

I've sent for help from all the Frankish lords.
We've got to drive away the Muslim hordes.

Richard Coeur de Lion

King Richard and King Philip said they'd come.
The Saracens should soon be on the run.

(Enter Philip).

Philip: Bonjour, mon brave! I'm Philip, King of France.
My army's here to help your men advance.

Besieging is my specialité:
We'll breech those Acre bulwarks any day!

Guy: Thank God you've come! We really need your aid.
But where is Richard? Has he been delayed?

Philip: I hear he stopped in Sicily en route.
He banged some heads and grabbed a load of loot.

He then set sail, but ran into a storm.
His ships were scattered and their sails were torn.

The last I heard he'd reached the Cyprus shore.
But what befell? We don't know any more.

Guy: The Lord of Cyprus is an awkward devil;
I hope that Richard's not in any peril.

I think I'd better go and see what's what,
While you stay here and rest -- it's very hot.

(Guy exits).

Philip: All right, but do come back from Cyprus fast.
Without more troops, this siege will never last.

Meanwhile, I cannot bear this blazing sun.
I'll have a snooze till Guy and Richard come.

(Philip settles down to sleep. Saladin peeps up over the castle wall).

Saladin: They say King Richard's strong and fearless. Ha!
Just wait until he sees my scimitar!

(Waves scimitar, then disappears. Philip crawls away. End of Act 2).

Act 3. Cyprus, near Limassol: May 1191.

(Enter Blondel, singing ♫ the first six couplets to any easy tune of the right metre (10.10.10.10) , eg a suitably adapted Finlandia by Sibelius).

Blondel: ♫ Now here I come, the minstrel Blondel. Why?
♫ To sing my master's praises to the sky!

♫ I'm good King Richard's fav'rite troubadour.
♫ I follow him about in time of war.

♫ And now we've come to Cyprus: what a trip!
♫ The storm was fierce; we nearly lost our ship.

♫ And that's not all: a hostile local lord
♫ Appeared and tried to put us to the sword!

♫ Richard was livid! Rounding up his band,
♫ He beat the Lord of Cyprus out of hand!

♫ The people now accept the English won,
♫ So we're collecting booty by the ton.

(Enter Guy, out of breath).

Guy: Ah, Blondell! I need Richard! Where is he?
I've come from Acre with an urgent plea.

Each day the Saracens are getting stronger.
And Philip can't maintain the siege much longer.

We need the English troops without delay.
So please can Richard take them there *today*!

Blondel: You're out of luck. He's on his honeymoon.
He married Berengaria at noon.

And hark! I hear the bridesmaids singing still!
Their gentle, dulcet tones give me a thrill!

(Off stage, female singing is heard. Enter Richard, with Berengaria on his arm).

Richard: What ho! Meet Berengaria, my bride.
This marriage thing I'm taking in my stride!

The Cyprus package-honeymooning style
Is great! I'll linger longer on this Isle!

Guy: Oh, no! He's going soft! ... This is disaster!
Soon Saladin will be King Richard's master!

Richard: What? Saladin defeat me? Never! Ever!
Come, Guy: let's hurry back to war together!

(Guy and Richard exit rapidly. Blondel looks with dismay and sympathy at the dejected Berengaria).

Blondel: The shortest honeymoon I've ever seen!
Small consolation that you're now a Queen.

Go back to England; wait there for your liege.
I'll follow him to Acre for the siege.

(Berengaria exits, followed shortly by Blondel. End of Act 3).

Act 4: At the siege of Acre again, June 1191.

(Enter Saladin, who stands in front of his castle).

Saladin: It's me again - still very much alive!
I hear that Richard shortly will arrive.

I'd like to meet this English popinjay
And see if he's as bold as people say.

I'm told his great two-handed sword can smash
A bar of iron with a single slash,

Whereas my trusty scimitar can slit
A velvet cushion at a single hit.

(Enter Richard, followed by Blondel, Philip & Guy. Saladin & Richard confront each other).

King Richard Coeur de Lion, I presume!
The Cross will give way to the Crescent-moon!

Richard: Ah, Saladin! We'll shortly see who's boss;
The Crescent must make way before the Cross!

(Saladin & Richard stand eye-ball to eye-ball).

Blondel: My Lords! I have a cushion and a bar.
So, try your strength. Let's see who is the star.

(Blondel gives the cushion to R. and the bar to S).

Richard: A cushion? Is that all you can afford?
I'll soon divide it with my mighty sword!

(Richard attempts to cut the cushion with his huge but relatively blunt sword).

Saladin : An Iron bar? You must be short of cash!
I'll soon divide it with a single slash!

(Saladin attempts to break the iron bar with his razor-sharp but light and flimsy scimitar).

Blondel: Two noble champions! See how they fight!
When East meets West, who knows which side is right?

(Saladin gives up trying, exhausted).

Saladin: I yield! The town of Acre now is yours,
If you agree to buzz off from these shores.

Richard: No! Not until Jerusalem I see.
Jerusalem's the place I want to be!

Guy: I cannot see us take Jerusalem.
I'd rather live in Cyprus -- there's a gem!

Richard: All right, have Cyprus, Guy. By me that's fine.
You're not the man to rule in Palestine.

(Guy exits).

I'll march to Jaffa, conquer it, and then
Turn inland, so to reach Jerusalem.

Philip: Well, I'll be going home. This blinding sun
Is really much too hot for anyone.

(Starts to exit, saying conspiratorially to the audience ...)

Besides, with Richard still out East crusading,
His lands in France are suitable for raiding!

(Philip exits).

Saladin: Your Frankish army's dwindling. Let's make peace.
We're both exhausted. Let the fighting cease.

Richard: I'll let you have your Palestinian bases
If you will still respect our Holy Places.

Saladin: I'll leave the Christian pilgrims well alone
If you agree to take your soldiers home.

Richard: All right. It's back to England. There's bad news.
Prince John's betrayed my trust -- no time to lose!

Come, Blondel. Let's set sail and take a chance
By trav'lling light, through Austria and France.

(Richard and Blondel exit speedily).

Saladin: Farewell, brave King! Good luck across the Med.
I pray for him, for trouble lies ahead.

(Saladin exits. End of Act 4).

Act 5: A castle somewhere in Germany, early spring 1193.

(The scene opens with Richard looking up over the walls of Colditz Castle, deep in the heart of Germany).

Richard: Disaster! What we thought an easy trip
Was ruined when some pirates took our ship!

I slipped away, and set off overland
Disguised, for safety, as a kitchen-hand.

But I was recognised and thrown in clink!
Unchivalrous behaviour, don't you think?

The German Duke, who started all this woe,
Demands some cash before he'll let me go.

They call this Colditz Castle. I don't care,
For what's far worse, my men don't know I'm here.

If only I could get a message through,
My friends would quickly pay the ransom due.

(Enter Blondel, singing ♫ the first four couplets to any easy tune of the right metre (10.10.10.10) , eg a suitably adapted Finlandia by Sibelius). Blondel does not notice Richard, until Richard joins in by singing the fifth couplet only, alone).

Blonde!: ♫ Now here I come, the minstrel Blondel. Why?
♫ To sing my master's praises to the sky!

♫ I'm good King Richard's fav'rite troubadour.
♫ I follow him about in time of war.

♫ And now I've come to Germany, to seek
♫ My master, who was caught the other week.

♫ And that's not all: a hostile local lord
♫ Appeared and tried to put him to the sword!

Richard: ♫ And I was livid! Lost without my band,
♫ They led me captive, chains around my hand....

Thank God you've come, good Blondel! ... I was sure
I'd languish in this keep for evermore.

Blondel: King Richard! I've been searching high and low!
I guessed that you'd been captured by the foe.

Your men in England long for your return.
There's treachery afoot, as you'll soon learn.

Richard: The chaps who hold me are a bunch of sharks.
My ransom is one hundred thousand marks!

Return to England. Go and raise the cash.
When free, I'll give my enemies a bash.

(Blondel exits).

I've enemies in England and in France
Who'd take my fiefdoms, given half a chance.

So, when the ransom's paid and I'm at large,
I'll show those scheming traitors who's in charge!

(Richard ducks down behind the castle wall, out of sight. Act 5 ends)

Act 6: The English court at London, March 1194.

(Enter Eleanor and Berengaria, looking miserable and consoling each other. Shortly after, enter Blondel singing ♫ the first two couplets to any easy tune of the right metre (10.10.10.10) , eg a suitably adapted Finlandia by Sibelius).
.

Blondel: ♫ Now here I come, the minstrel Blondel. Why?
♫ To sing my master's praises to the sky!

♫ I'm good King Richard's fav'rite troubadour.
♫ I follow him about in time of war.

I bring good news! King Richard's free at last!
The randsom's paid; he's fit, and trav'lling fast.

He's frightened Philip into backing down,
So Philip now respects the Ang'vin crown.

Eleanor: I'm glad to hear it! Now perhaps Prince John
Will come to heel. .... Support for him has gone.

I'll send Queen Berengaria to Dover
To welcome home our bold Crusading rover.

(Exit Berengaria).

Blondel: As Richard travelled home through Normandy
The Frankish people welcomed him with glee.

(Noises of cheering are heard off stage).

And now I hear the cheers go up and down:
King Richard is approaching London Town!

(Enter Richard, with Berengaria looking happy on his arm).

Richard: Hi, Mum! You haven't altered in the least
Whilst I've been off Crusading in the East.

I'm glad to say the Holy Land's at peace,
And France is calm and Frankish squabbles cease.

But what of England? How are things back here?
Prince John has been oppressing you, I fear.

Blondel: Oh, Sire! The people suffer ev'ry day.
But now all's well, for John has gone away.

Richard: I pardon all of those who did you wrong;
And I forgive my little brother John.

And, knowing that they laboured to do good,
I thank such loyal folk as Robin Hood.

('Huray!' is heard off stage).

Eleanor: Although your absences from home were long,
We all affirm: 'To England you belong!'

In foreign lands you played a hero's part:
So we'll remember Richard Lionheart!

(Cheers are heard off stage. All bow to Richard, who strikes a heroic pose).

End.

A7. Good Queen Bess *or how to survive religion, politics and sex.*

Cast, in order of appearance.

Nursey	the royal nurse at Hampton Court Palace
Earl of Essex	a beau at Court
Queen Elizabeth I	
Sir Francis Drake	
Mary Queen of Scots	cousin of Elizabeth
Duke of Medina Sidona	a Spanish diplomat

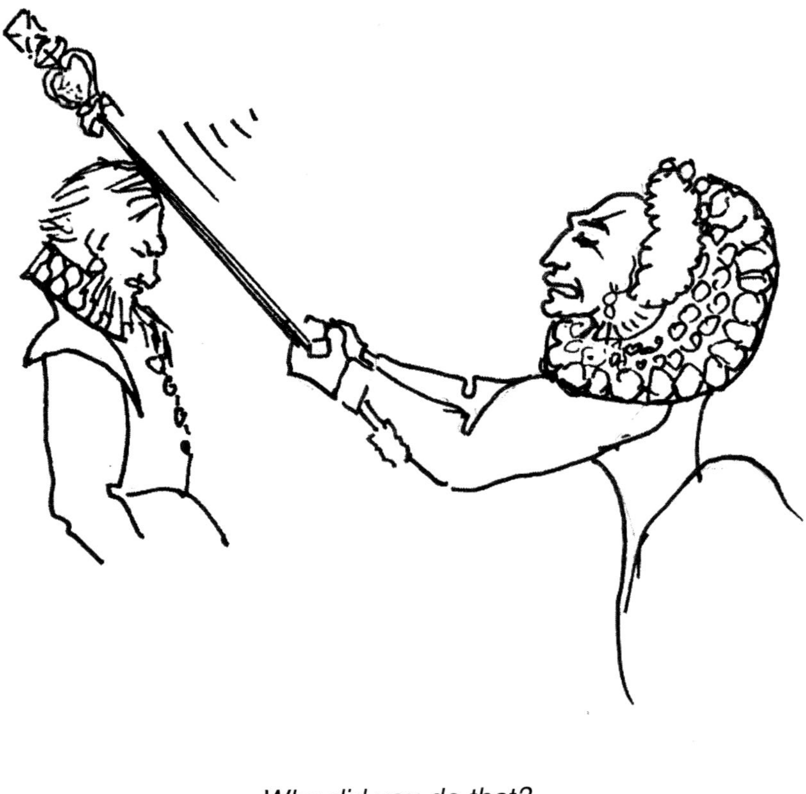

Why did you do that?

Good Queen Bess

The play is in four Acts, spanning the years 1558 to 1598.

Act 1: Hampton Court Palace, 1558.

(Enter Nursey).

Nursey: Now here come I, the trusty royal nurse.
In Tudor England, few jobs could be worse!

For looking after children at the court
Is certainly with many dangers fraught.

King Henry had three offspring. Two are dead.
I feared the third, my Bess, would lose her head.

Her mother, Anne Boleyn, was made much shorter
Because, instead of sons, she had a daughter!

But fate was kind. And now ... a marv'llous thing:
For yesterday my Bess became the Queen!

If only she can keep her pretty head
And, most of all, she mustn't ever wed.

For once she marries, all she's gained is loss
Because the man, in time, becomes the boss.

(Enter Essex, his cod-piece much in evidence)

Essex: Now here come I, Earl Essex, beau at Court.
I'm known for being excellent at sport.

Round here, the only sport we like to play
Is 'chase the ladies' .... ardently ... each day!

At Hampton Court we lads come up a-prancing
And charm the ladies with our sexy dancing.

(makes suggestive hip wriggles).

Until they sing 'Hey nonny nonny No!'
With many-a wink and nod we let them go.

That young Elizabeth's a dainty dish.
To have her as my bride's my ardent wish!

Nursey: Oh, fie, my Lord, you are a saucy fellow.
Come, don't you fancy something plump and mellow?

(Essex eyes Nursey's ample bosom).

But wait! Her royal highness comes this way!
Let's save these frolics for another day.

(Enter Elizabeth, with sceptre).

Eliz.: Now here come I, Elizabeth, your Queen!
The brand new sov'reign of this England green.

These last few years of politics and plot
Have terrified the people quite a lot.

Extreme religious dogma is the source
Of all the instability, of course.

It's time we had some tolerance and peace.
Let argument and foreign meddling cease!

My dad, Henry the eighth, was right indeed:
The Church of England's all we ever need.

The Pope declares our Church is very lax.
So what? That's fine! … Why don't we all relax?

Essex: Your majesty, I have the self-same thought!
So let's relax and play a little sport.

Away, old Nursey! These are things of State.
The Queen and I have matters to debate.

(Nursey exits, smirking to herself. Essex begins to cuddle a not-unwilling Elizabeth, but they are soon interrupted. Enter Drake).

Good Queen Bess

Drake: Now here come I, the bold Sir Francis Drake.
I've sailed the seven seas -- and no mistake!

My ship, the *Golden Hind*, has found much gain
By plund'ring up and down the Spanish Main.

Essex: Who wants to know about your Gold Behind?
We've more important things at Court, you'll find.

Drake: No, wait! I come to warn your Majesty:
The Spanish plan to dominate the sea.

Their ships are large and pow'rful. ... I predict
That if it comes to war, they'll have us licked.

Our navy's rather small - we need to build
A lot more ships, or else we'll all be killed.

Essex: We don't believe your silly information.
Our plans are adequate to save the nation.

You smell of fish! Stop making all this fuss!
Begone! And leave the politics to us!

(Drake exits looking angry & frustrated)

We were *relaxed* before that fish-head came;
So let's resume our cuddly game again!

(Essex tries to embrace Elizabeth. She waves her sceptre at him, and he tries playfully to take it away from her).

Eliz.: I have a headache, Essex! Go away!
We'll play your sport again another day.

Unhand me, sir! I'm off to have a nap;
I'll keep my sceptre firmly on my lap.

(Elizabeth exits, clutching her sceptre to her stomach)

Essex: The lady teases me! Yet I don't mind.
I'll have her in a while; I know her kind!

(Essex exits, smirking)

Act 2. Somewhere in the North of England, after 1567.

(Enter Mary)

Mary: Now here come I, I'm Mary, Queen of Scots.
Of husbands and of troubles I've had lots.

At first I married Francis, King of France.
But when he died, I felt I'd lost a chance.

For he and I were Cath'lics through and through,
And wished to make all Scotland Cath'lic too.

My second husband didn't last too long:
My lover sent him packing with a bomb!

My lover caused the Scots to throw me out,
So now I've come down South to sow some doubt.

For England's largely Protestant right now,
But soon I'll make it Catholic, I vow!

My cousin Bess has never been my pal -
She thinks I'm just a frenchman's good-time girl.

I'll show Elizabeth a thing or two,
That prissy little skinny virgin - pooh!

(Enter Medina).

Medina: Now here come I, the Spanish Duke Medina.
I serve King Philip - and there's no-one keener.

And, as Ambassador, it is my duty
To stir up trouble --- Ah! Hello, my beauty!

(Notices Mary & is enchanted)

Aren't you the hope of ev'ry Cath'lic heart?
Perhaps a revolution we can start?

The Pope has dealt Elizabeth a blast
And excommunicated her at last.

The Pope would like her kingdom overthrown -
I'm doubtful you can do it on your own,

But Spain will come and give a helping hand.
Let's plan a revolution in this land.

Mary: Ambassador: I'd like to join your plot.
For cousin Bess I do not care a jot!

Her "Church" of England's an abomination.
With Spanish help, we'll overthrow this nation!

(Enter Essex, with a dramatic flourish)

Essex: Hold hard! I come from Hampton in the west.
I have a warrant here for your arrest!

The Queen commands that you should be detained
So all your Cath'lic plots may be constrained.

It's off to prison. I'm to be your guard –
A task I'm sure I won't find very hard!

(Essex clutches Mary lustfully round the waist; Mary yields not unwillingly & they exit together).

Medina: Well, that's the end of one potential scheme –
Perhaps the end of Mary, it would seem?

. No matter: other plans come on apace,
For soon a great invasion will take place.

We've many ships and many troops prepared,
So England has good reason to be scared.

In Spain a huge Armada is assembling.
That Queen Elizabeth - she should be trembling!

Soon Spanish Dukes will rule this England green,
Then who will save their precious Virgin Queen?!

(Medina exits with an evil leer).

Act 3: London, summer 1588.

(Enter Elizabeth, comforted by Nursey)

Nursey: There, there, my dear: now don't you be upset,
For Scots and English *might* be allies yet.

Your cousin Mary plotted round the clock.
You *had* to have her head upon the block.

Eliz.: I s'pose you're right. But still, it makes me cry
Each time a *relative* of mine must die.

Her death will teach a lesson to the French;
And, after all, she *was* a scheming wench!

Although I know my soldiers chopped her head,
I wish they'd killed some foreigners instead.

(Enter Medina with a letter. He bows extravagantly and awaits Elizabeth's attention)

And talking, by the way, of foreign scum,
I see the Spanish diplomat has come.

(Elizabeth takes the letter & reads it)

Medina: Your majesty! I bring the gravest news.
We're now at war, and I've no time to lose.

I'm off to join the Spanish fleet at sea.
And Spain will win a famous victory!

(Medina bows excessively, and exits)

Nursey: We're in for trouble now! Our ships are small,
And in a battle we've no chance at all!

Eliz. You may be right. I wish that Drake was here
To re-assure us and to give us cheer.

(Elizabeth flourishes the letter)

The King of Spain is planning to invade us!
He means to conquer England and degrade us.

(Enter Drake, out of breath).

Drake: Your majesty! I come from Plymouth strand.
We've spied the Great Armada close to land!

Prepare the Fort at Tilb'ry for invasion!
Let's reinforce the troops for this occasion!

Your Highness, let's assemble on the beech
And liven up the soldiers with a speech.

(Elizabeth steps forward and addresses the audience, as if they were the English troops assembled at Tilbury Fort).

Eliz: My loving, loyal people gathered here,
Let's all be brave! And let the tyrants fear!

I am resolved, in battle if I must,
To live and die amongst you in the dust.

And, though I'm braced to face the Spanish raid,
You see I have the body of a maid.

But deep inside this weak and feeble thing
There lies the heart and stomach of a king!

A King of England! And I think foul scorn
That any foreign prince of mother born

Should dare invade the borders of my realm –
Especially now that Drake is at the helm!

I do not doubt that vict'ry will be ours!
We'll not be ruled by any foreign powers!

(Cheers are heard from the troops)

Drake: Bravo! At times like this we surely need
A Queen like you to give us all a lead.

I'm off to join my ship at Plymouth Hoe.
Our men are well-prepared to meet the foe.

(Drake exits)

Nursey: Farewell, Sir Francis! May you safe return.
Until you come, my heart for you will yearn.

(Elizabeth & Nursey exit, comforting each other. Drums roll. There are flashes and the sound of gunfire).

Act 4: Hampton Court Palace, 1598.

(Enter Essex. His clothes are no longer smart).

Essex: It's 40 years since Bess began to reign
And here I am at Hampton Court again.

The nation thrives. We won the Spanish War.
And all the proud Armada is no more.

Sir Francis Drake, the hero of the hour,
Has grown in honour, favour, wealth and power.

The Queen remains as active as before,
Whilst I decline! Oh, life is such a bore!

She doesn't fancy me - or any beau.
And is she still a virgin? Who would know?

She sent me off to Ireland for a spell,
And there I had some rioting to quell.

And, now I'm back, I find that I'm ignored.
No wonder chaps like me are getting bored!

It's time for change. Queen Bess has reigned too long.
The way she treats her men is very wrong.

Although the mass of people all adore her,
Some Catholics in England still deplore her.

(Nursey creeps in unobserved, and overhears Essex. She gasps in amazement at the impending treachery)

I hear of lots of plots to take the throne.
I think I'll join the move to sack the crone.

(Essex is pre-occupied; he does not see or hear Nursey).

Nursey: My goodness! I can scarce believe a word!
I'd better tell Sir Francis what I've heard.

(Nursey creeps out).

Essex: The time has come when I should strut my stuff
And show that Essex lads have had enough!

The road to civil war I'll now ascend,
For Virgin Bess deserves a sticky end!

(Drake and Nursey rush in. Drake has a drawn sword and confronts Essex fiercely. Nursey has a rope).

Drake: Enough of that! ... Arrest the trait'rous cad!
I always knew that gents like you were bad!

(Nursey ties Essex's hands in front of him).

You lounge around the Palace like a lizard.
I've half a mind to slit your flabby gizzard!

'Affairs of State' to you are but a game;
And now betrayal! ... What? Have you no shame?

(Enter Elizabeth, looking majestic).

Eliz.: Aha! I see you've caught that scheming man.
I'd heard that he had hatched an evil plan.

The time has come when I prefer him dead.
Cut off his cod-piece, then cut off his head!

(Essex exits looking terrified, clutching his cod-piece. Drake pushes Essex off, & then comforts Nursey).

So die all traitors. Ev'ryone be warned:
There's none so vengeful as a woman scorned!

It's thanks to people such as Drake and Nurse
That we've survived invasion, plots, and worse.

(Drake and Nursey put a friendly arm around each other)

It's also thanks to good old Nurse and Drake
That ruling England's now a piece of cake.

The moral of this tale is plain to see:
Successful monarchs operate like me.

(She flourishes her sceptre suggestively)

If you would be *Regina*, or a *Rex*,
Avoid religion, politics and sex!

End.

A8. The Belle of Naples *or The Immortal Memory***.**

Cast, in order of appearance.

Annabel,	Lady Emma's maid.
King Ferdinand IV,	King of the Two Sicilies, including all of Italy south of Rome.
Sir William Hamilton	British Ambassador to the Court of the Two Sicilies in Naples.
Lady Emma Hamilton,	famed for her beauty.
Billy Hoste,	a young Midshipman in Nelson's ships.
Horatio Nelson,	British naval hero.
Two British sailors	*(The sailors only come on in the last Act. They have nothing to say. They can be played by Sir William and the King, who are both dead before the final Act).*

Sigh!

Belle of Naples

The action of this five-Act play takes place between 1793 and 1805, mainly in the Naples house of Sir William Hamilton. The last Act takes place in Gibraltar, just after the Battle of Trafalgar.

Act 1: 1793, at the Naples house of Sir William Hamilton.

(Enter Annabel, with broom).

Annabel: Now here come I, I'm Annabel the maid.
I'm highly prized, although I'm lowly paid.

For I'm the eyes and ears of Naples Bay.
I like to know what's happening each day –

Like 'Who is doing what, to whom, and why'.
There's few intrigues that simply pass me by.

This mansion is the British Embassy –
The finest house in southern Italy.

I serve the Lady Emma Hamilton,
Which actu'lly is sometimes rather fun.

She's married to Sir William. What a life!
For Emma is Sir William's second wife.

An Artist's Model was her former trade,
And she was never slow at getting laid!

But then Sir William Hamilton gave chase,
And married her, and took her to this place.

But he is over sixty, so I'm told,
Whilst Emma's only twenty nine years old.

(Enter King Ferdinand. Annabel sidles into a corner, pretending to sweep).

Ferdinand: Now here come I, King Ferdinand the Fourth.
I rule Italian lands both south and north.

But here in Naples is my special spot:
The sun, the sand, the booze, the girls - the lot!

Of all the local talent on the beach,
That sexy kitten, Emma, is the peach!

This Embassy's my fav'rite stamping-ground:
It's here the gorgeous Emma can be found ...

(He notices Annabel for the first time).

Brace up there, girl! Don't stand around all day!
Tell Emma that the King has come to play!

Annabel: Your Highness, Emma's not at home right now ....

(Aside, to the audience)

She may not like your playing, anyhow.

And be advised: Sir William's coming here.
He may not like the games you play: take care!

(Enter Sir William)

Sir William: Now here come I, Sir William Hamilton:
The grandest British diplomat, bar none!

Of politics I may not know a lot,
But as for art and culture: I'm red hot!

Collecting Roman statues is my hobby -
You may have seen them mounted in the lobby.

Antiquities round here? There is no dearth.
This Bay of Naples? - Paradise on earth!

I like a bit of beauty in my life,
And as for beauty, you should see my wife!

(Aside, to the audience:)

I rather think King Ferdie likes her face,
And that is why he hovers round this place.

But I don't mind. King Ferdie has his uses.
He's free to chat up Emma when he chooses.

Ferdinand: Hello, Sir William, what's the latest rumour?
I hope you won't deflate my mellow humour!

Sir William: I hear the French and English are at war.
So England's fighting for its life once more.

But here in Naples, we have got it made:
The French are hardly likely to invade.

Ferdinand: My family are Bourbons. We're the best!
The rest of Europe bows at our behest!

The French won't dare to threaten our estate –
And if they do, then we'll ... negotiate!

(Enter Billy Hoste hesitatingly. Annabel is immediately rather taken by the young Midshipman. Annabel encourages him to speak up).

Billy: Now here come I, Midshipman Billy Hoste;
When duty calls, I'm always at my post!

I'm coming from Gibraltar, just today;
You'll see our vessel anchored in the Bay.

My Captain has dispatches from the war.
He seeks a meeting with th'Ambassador.

(Billy looks enquiringly from one to another.)

Sir William: Well, I am he. Pray, what's your captain's name?
And is he well-connected? What's his claim?

Billy: He has no title, nor a country seat,
But he's the bravest Captain in the fleet.

He's been at sea since he was aged thirteen.
He's small of stature, but he's very keen.

His name is Captain Nelson. He's the best!
There's none to match his courage, east or west!

Sir William: I don't know any Nelsons, I declare!
I s'pose I'd better see him. Fetch him here!

(Billy & Annabel exit; Sir William turns to King F.)

Excuse us: these dispatches are a bore!
This won't take long - and then we'll talk some more.

(King Ferdinand exits).

I wonder what's the news this Captain's got?
I hope he won't disturb our peaceful spot.

Enter Nelson with a letter, followed by Billy and Annabel).

Nelson: Now here come I, and Nelson is my name,
And victory for Britain is my aim!

(First addresses Billy and Annabel, and then addresses Sir William)

Please leave us .... .. I have grave and urgent news
About the war. I seek Sir William's views.

(Billy and Annabel leave, but Annabel creeps back unseen, to listen. Nelson hands Sir William the letter. Sir William reads it, looking worried).

You'll see the French are gaining strength this year.
They plan to conquer Italy, we hear.

Can you persuade the weak King Ferdinand
To raise an army and defend his land?

If Naples falls, the French will dominate
The Mediterranean, ... at any rate.

And now Napoleon's the boss of France,
He'll lead the rest of Europe quite a dance.

So ... my advice to Ferdinand is plain:
'Prepare for war, or face defeat and shame'.

And now, farewell! I sail without delay.
I'll bring you news again another day.

(Nelson exits with a flourish. As he goes out, we hear him shout:)

Midshipman! Call my boat-crew to the quay.
This place is much too decadent for me!

Sir William: Well, what a brash young man, that Nelson chap!
Can he be right, or is he talking crap?

Napoleon is certainly a threat,
But would he scoop up Naples in his net?

I'd better talk to Ferdie. Though he's weak
And will not fight, some compromise he'll seek.

(Sir William exits. Annabel emerges from her hiding-place).

Annabel: I hardly think Sir William's comprehended
That times of luxury and ease have ended.

I bet the French will conquer Italy.
And then they're sure to sack this Embassy.

And then we'll all evacuate to Malta –
Or else we'll seek a refuge in Gibraltar.

(Enter Emma).

Emma: Now here come I, I'm Emma Hamilton -
When I'm around, there's sure to be some fun!

Although Sir William is a pompous bore,
He tolerates my fancies more and more.

What's this I hear about a Malta trip?
That sounds like fun, so lead me to the ship!

Annabel: Oh, no, my Lady. There's no trip today.
That is a British *warship* in the bay.

She brought us messages of gloom and doom.
Her Captain has this minute left the room.

Emma: I *thought* I heard strange voices in the hall.
Who was that earnest man who came to call?

Annabel: His name is Captain Nelson. He's a star.
Though rather young, he'll certainly go far.

Emma: A young man who'll go far? For that I pray!
I hope he calls again another day!

Annabel: And as for that Midshipman: he's a cutie!
I hope he comes again to do his duty!

(Annabel and Emma exit, wistfully).

Act 2: Naples, a few months later.

(Enter Sir William, briefly displaying a placard that says: "Act 2: a few months later". After showing it to the audience, he discards it, pauses a few moments, and then says:).

Sir William: I wonder where that Nelson fellow is?
He hasn't called for months, so what's his biz?

Perhaps his bold, but rather tactless, trend
Has caused the man to meet a sticky end!

(Enter Billy, with Nelson close behind; Nelson has a patch over his right eye and a medal on his chest.).

Billy: Make way for Nelson, coming from the war.
He's now promoted to a Commodore!

Sir William: But what has happened to your covered eye?
Pray, tell us of the battle; don't be shy.

Nelson: I lost it in the fight for Corsica.
The Frenchies got away, but not too far.

When they return, they'll have a lot more ships,
And then the Med. will come within their grips.

But what about your friend King Ferdinand?
Has he decided to defend his land?

Sir William: Oh, Ferdie's taken fright and gone away.
I shouldn't count on his support today.

Nelson: Soon England will become the only one
To stand against that rogue Napoleon.

I fear that Spain will give the French their backing.
It won't be long till Naples gets a whacking.

(Enter Emma and Annabel. Annabel only has eyes for Billy. Emma is entranced by Nelson).

Emma: Who is this one-eyed naval officer?
And, William, why's he causing such a stir?

Sir William: Forgive me, Emma. May I now present
Horatio Nelson. He's a ... Naval gent.

Emma: Horatio! Gosh, what a rousing name!
I've heard about your battles and your fame.

(Nelson bows & is mildly embarrassed).

Nelson: I'm charmed to meet you, Ma'am, but I must go.
We sail without delay to meet the foe.

Sir William: What? Off again? I'd better wave goodbye.
I must admit, Nelson, you're quite a guy!

(Nelson exits with a flourish, with Billy and Sir William not far behind. As he goes out, we hear Nelson shout:)

Nelson: Midshipman! Call my boat-crew to the quay.
This Emma is too beautiful for me.

(Emma and Annabel remain side by side, waving farewell to the departing Nelson and Billy).

Emma: Oh, what a brave and dashing sailor man!
If anyone can fight, Horatio can!

Annabel: Oh! What a brave and dashing sailor boy!
Midshipman Billy: you're my pride and joy!

And England needs such men in times of war –
And they'll soon give Napoleon *What For!*

Emma: When they're not fighting, they'll have time to play!
I hope they call again another day!

(Exit Emma and Annabel. End of Act 2).

Act 3: Naples, a few months later.

(Enter Emma and Annabel. Emma briefly displays a placard that says: "Act 3: a few months later". After showing it to the audience, she discards it, pauses a few moments, and then says:).

Emma: In Naples, life has turned to gloom and doom.
The people say the French are coming soon.

Supplies are short: we're all on rations now.
But never mind - we'll manage anyhow!

Annabel: Well, things have surely gone from bad to worse;
I'm volunteering as a part-time nurse.

King Ferdie's done a bunk - no more pretences.
So who will organise the town's defences?

Emma: Sir William's busy hiding his antiques --
That's all he's thought about for weeks and weeks –

And so, I guess, it's really up to me,
Though how effective can I hope to be?

(Enter Billy, followed by Nelson. The right-hand coat-sleeve of Nelson's tunic is empty and is pinned up to indicate that his arm has been amputated. He wears more medals).

Billy: Make way for Nelson: everybody shall!
He's now promoted to an Admiral.

Emma: But what has happened to your poor right arm?
I weep to see that you have come to harm.

Nelson: I lost it in the fight for Santa Cruz –
The action was a muddle - no excuse.

If Billy here had not been by my side
To act as shield, I'm sure I would have died.

Billy: But it was *you* who led us in the fray.
We'll follow you to vict'ry any day!

Annabel: Come, Billy, tell me all the dreadful story
Of how you came to grips with death or glory.

(Annabel & Billy exit, arm in arm. Thus left alone, Emma and Nelson start to become intimate).

Emma: You dear, dear man! You need a thorough rest.
Please stay with us in Naples as our guest.

Nelson: With you to nurse me, Emma? Oh, what bliss ....

Emma: I'll start the cure directly ... . with a kiss!

(They kiss briefly, but Nelson slowly backs regretfully away).

Nelson: I'd really love to stay, but I'm afraid
The French fleet have evaded our blockade.

I need to catch them, but on this occasion
We really do not know their destination.

Napoleon and his army are on board;
To let the French escape we can't afford.

So is it Egypt, Greece or Sicily?
If India, then Egypt is the key.

Midshipman! .....

(Annabel & Billy enter rapidly, still arm in arm).

.... Call my boat-crew to the quay.
This Emma is the only one for me!

(Nelson exits gleefully & Billy follows. Emma & Annabel wave them off).

Emma: Goodbye, my darling! May you have success!
And come back soon and yield to my caress.

Annabel: Goodbye, sweet Billy. Keep him safe from harm.
Remember that he's only got one arm!

Emma: Oh, Annabel, and will this bloody war
So dominate our lives for evermore?

Annabel: Young Billy told me more of Nelson's story:
It's not all action, cannon-fire and glory.

For Nelson's health is not robust - it's waning.
He finds each fight emotionally draining.

He has a wife, but they are now apart;
They weren't exactly cosy from the start.

He needs a woman's calming and support.
If you can help him, then I think you ought.

Emma: I love that Admir'l. What else can I say?
I hope he calls again another day!

(Emma and Annabel exit, wistfully. End of Act 3).

Act 4: Naples, a few months later.

(Enter Sir William, followed by Emma and Annabel. Sir William briefly displays a placard that says: "Act 4: a few months later". After showing it to the audience, he discards it, pauses a few moments, and then says:).

Sir William: Now Naples is besieged. How most alarming!
The prospect of a fight is far from charming.

A battle zone is not the place for me.
I'd better plan to leave quite soon by sea.

I'll pack my precious art in boxes stout
And hope a British ship can take them out.

(Sir William exits, looking worried).

Emma: I fear Sir William hasn't got a clue.
If Nelson came, *he'd* know just what to do!

I never thought that things would reach this state.
On England's Navy hangs all Europe's fate.

(Enter Billy, followed by Nelson who has a bandaged head and obviously looks in need of a good rest. He wears yet more medals).

Billy: Make way for Baron Nelson: bow the knee!
He's now promoted to the C-in-C.

Our Navy's won a great and glorious battle;
We gave Napoleon a thorough rattle!

Emma: But what has happened to your wounded head?
My dearest darling! You should be in bed!

Billy and Annabel: go fetch a drink.

(Billy and Annabel go out, tittering. Emma turns to Nelson).

Come, sit down here and let us have a think.

(Emma sits down on a couch, inviting Nelson to sit beside her. As the play proceeds, they gradually cuddle and lie down, until they are well and truly intimate).

Nelson: We caught the French in Egypt, near the Nile.
The Med's now free of Frenchmen for a while.

. But their Atlantic fleet is still at sea,
And Spain will add to this, it seems to me.

If we can't sink the French and Spanish fleet
Then England will, before long, face defeat.

Emma: Don't talk too much! You need to rest your head.
You must admit: this *is* a comfy bed!

(They both cuddle down together).

You dear, brave man! ... Enough of gun and sword.
Come to my arms and get your just reward!

Nelson: My dearest Em: I've been at sea too long!
Though parts of me are weak, some parts are strong!

(Sounds of heavy breathing soon subside, as they doze off to sleep in a mutual embrace. After a decent interval, enter Billy and Annabel with much diplomatic clearing of throats. Annabel holds a bottle; Billy holds one small packet and one large envelope).

Billy: Er ... Admiral: I've brought you this French letter!
Please keep it by you, then I'll feel much better.

(Billy hands the embarrassed Nelson a little packet which looks just like a contraceptive (which it is!). Nelson tucks it into his pocket quickly).

And here's another, captured by our ship.
I guess we're now required to make a trip?

(Nelson and Emma stand up and re-arrange their dress. Nelson takes the larger letter from Billy and reads it).

Nelson: Bad news. I've Orders from the Adm'ralty.
They say we've quickly got to put to sea.

The French are nearing England, to invade,
And I must sail to stop them, by blockade.

Farewell! I hope to see you in Gibraltar.
And, Emma dear, our love will never falter.

(Nelson and Emma embrace passionately. Annabel and Billy embrace discretely).

Farewell to you, my own true love, my beauty!
England expects that I will do my duty!

Midshipman! Call my boat-crew to the quay.
This place has given strength and hope to me!

(Nelson and Billy exit. Emma sighs, and stares longingly after Nelson. Annabel turns to the audience).

Annabel: They're both in love! We shouldn't say too much,
For Emma's surely felt the Nelson touch!

(Enter Sir William, in a rush, from the opposite direction).

Sir William: Oh blast! I've missed him! Quickly, to the bay!
We'll get aboard his ship without delay.

We can't stay here. He'll take us to Gibraltar.
The French are near at hand, so do not falter.

(Sir William rushes out, followed quickly by an alarmed Emma and Annabel. End of Act 4).

Act 5: In Gibraltar, a couple of years later.

(Enter Emma and Annabel. Emma looks worn out with care, but Annabel is doing her best to keep their spirits up. Emma briefly displays a placard that says: 'Act 5: a couple of years later, in Gibraltar'. After showing it to the audience, she discards it, pauses a few moments, and then says:).

Emma: We've watched and waited here at Gib. for ages,
Whilst up and down the tide of conflict rages.

Sir William died last year and left me lonely.
I'm friendless here, except for Anna only.

Our wealth is nearly gone: we're refugees.
These troubled times have brought us to our knees.

Annabel: Well, Nelson's still been sending lots of letters;
I'm confident that Nelson won't forget us.

Emma: The French and Spanish fleets have put to sea
The other day, so where can Nelson be?

Annabel: Some British frigates came, and from their crews
Just yesterday I had some cheering news:

The British, led by Nelson, came a-dashing.
The French and Spanish fleets will get a thrashing!

The *Victory's* the name of Nelson's ship,
And victory's on ev'ry sailor's lip.

It's Cape Trafalgar where the battle rages –
The greatest, fiercest, naval fight for ages.

Emma: The British fleet's out-numbered in this strife.
Though he's so brave, I fear for Nelson's life.

Annabel: Though Nelson is out-numbered, he'll survive.
He'll win the battle, and return alive!

(Sound of solemn drum-beat. Enter Billy, much distraught with grief, followed by two sailors carrying the be-medalled corpse of Nelson. They lay the corpse gently down mid-stage on a couch. Billy, overcome with grief, starts to speak hesitantly, in solemn prose).

Billy : Make way .... for the body .... of my dearest friend ... and our victorious leader .... Admiral ... Viscount ... Horatio ... Nelson.

(Annabel and Emma cry out in grief. The two sailors stand with bowed heads in the background, as if guarding the body).

Emma: Horatio! Horatio, my dear!
This grief, my own true love, I cannot bear!

(Emma collapses, quietly sobbing, onto Nelson's body and buries her head on his breast).

Annabel: Dear Emma! Let your hero gently lie.
And, sweetest Billy, *please* try not to cry.

(Annabel puts an arm round Billy, who recovers himself and puts on a brave face again).

Billy: Oh, I've survived unscathed, though hundreds died –
But most of them were on the other side.

For Nelson led our fleet to victory.
And England from invasion's threat is free!

Annabel: But how did Nelson die? How did he fall?
Was it by sword, or else by cannon ball?

Billy: At battle's height, above the roar, one crack!
A deadly sniper's bullet broke his back.

I cradled him below, on bended knee.
And, as he died, he said these words to me:

"I thank the Lord that I have done my duty.
And, Billy, take these kisses to my beauty".

(Billy blows a kiss towards the recumbent Emma and Nelson).

Annabel: Those two adored each other's company.
The moral of this tale is plain to me:

Be they so brave and fearless whilst afloat,
All sailors need a girl on which to dote!

(Billy and Annabel embrace).

Billy: Trafalgar proved the end for foreign knaves.
Britannia's now the ruler of the waves!

From this day forth, then, let us all remember
Our brave Lord Nelson and his lovely Emma.

As long as Britons sail across the sea,
We'll all salute th' Immortal Memory!

(The two sailors come to life, and cheer, as do Billy and Annabel. Nelson and Emma remain as if dead).

End.

A9. Eleanor of Aquitaine.

Cast, in order of appearance.

Eleanor of Aquitaine
King Louis of France
Chevalier Maurice, attended by French knights.
Henry, Duke of Normandy, later Henry II King of England.
Sir Edmund, attended by English knights.
Prince Richard Coeur de Lion, son of Henry & Eleanor, later Richard I King of England.
Prince John, son of Henry & Eleanor, later John King of England.

Mine, all mine!

Eleanor of Aquitaine

The action takes place at various locations in western Europe between 1137 and 1204. There are five Acts.

Act 1. Approximately 1137 – 1150.

(Enter Eleanor)

Eleanor: Now here come I, I'm Eleanor, whose fame
Is known beyond my State of Aquitaine.

I'm aged fifteen -- a Duchess! Fancy that!
But forced to marry Louis: what a prat!

(Enter Louis)

Louis: Now here come I, King Louis number seven.
My modest kingdom's hardly made in heaven.

I *should* be King of *all* the Frankish lands
But half of these are now in other's hands.

Alas, from Flanders all the way to Spain
There's Dukes and Counts positioning for gain.

My ancestor, King Charlemagne the Great
Ruled *all* of Europe as a single state.

I wish that Europe once again could be
United with a single king – that's me!

Eleanor: Poor Louis' seeking easy ways to win
More land to rule. And here's where *I* come in.

By marry'ng me he thinks he'll thus obtain
My huge and wealthy State of Aquitaine.

(Louis lustily grabs Eleanor's hand and pulls her towards him).

But – not so fast! Although you've got my hand
We'll need a son before you'll rule *my* land.

Let's see some spirit, weedy little boy!
I'm now your Queen. I'm not your trophy toy!

Louis: All right, my love, I'll show you that I'm strong.
The next Crusade's all set. Let's string along.

(French knights enter, dressed as Crusaders and led by Chevalier Maurice).

I fancy fighting for a nobler cause
Instead of Europe's little local wars.

Maurice: Now here come I, Chevalier Maurice,
A bold French knight in wartime and in peace.

My job's to stiffen up the weak King Lou.
Let's go Crusading with this Frankish crew.

(The French knights start making typical French background noises.)

French: Alors! Tout suite! Quelle Force de Frappe!
Formidable! Etc. etc.

Louis: All right, we'll make a Holy Pilgrimage ....
And hope I won't get hurt when battles rage.

(Maurice and the French withdraw, still muttering, dragging Louis. Louis tries to drag Eleanor, who is slow to exit).

Eleanor: You must be tough to go on a Crusade.
Have you the blood and guts to make the grade?

Though you're a wimp, it *might* turn out all right:
Let's see if I can teach you how to fight!

And, anyway, there's more fish in the sea.
I'm very rich. Who knows who'll rescue me?

(Eleanor exits, waving enigmatically to the audience).

Act 2. Approximately 1150 – 1162.

(Enter Henry)

Henry: I'm Henry, Duke of Normandy, that's who!
And, through my fam'ly line, I rule Anjou.

The Anj'vin Empire's growing by degrees.
My aim is to expand it overseas

To England northwards, where my future lies,
As soon as wicked Uncle Stephen dies.

(English knights, led by Sir Edmund, come in quietly behind Henry).

For Grandpapa King Henry number one,
Was King of England - firmly on *that* throne!

Edmund: Now here come I, Sir Edmund, English knight.
Though he's half French, our Henry's quite all right.

The bad King Stephen's popped his clogs, poor thing,
So Henry here can now become our King.

(English now start shouting, like football supporters)

English: Two, four, six, eight: who do we appreciate?
Henry! ... Henry number two! Henry the Second!
Henry the Second, King of England! ... Hurray!

Henry: Well, thank you, fans! And now, for further gain,
Can I expand my empire south -- to Spain?

If only Duchess Eleanor were free,
I'd wed her. Then her lands would come to me.

When Louis grabbed her, Oh, I missed my chance!
For Aquitaine is now allied to France.

(Commotion off stage, French shouting. Enter Eleanor pursued by Maurice and French knights who try to hold her back. She breaks free.)

Eleanor: Oh, Henry! Help me! Louis' thrown me out
And all these French will kill me, there's no doubt.

Maurice: Crusading proved a failure from the start,
For Eleanor and Louis split apart.

And *she* was all for fighting with the fray
Whilst *he* just tried to hide and run away.

Now Louis has divorced poor Eleanor
So has she got a future anymore?

(Eleanor rushes into Henry's arms. They gaze into each other's eyes; It is love at first sight. Meanwhile, the English knights menace the French knights and frighten them off stage).

Edmund: Clear off, you Frenchies! Leave the lady be.
Fair Eleanor: relax, 'cos now you're free.

(Maurice and the French knights exit looking sheepish, pursued by English knights. Edmund remains on stage).

Eleanor: Dear Henry! Marry me without delay:
I'd rather you than Frenchmen any day!

Take me and Aquitaine: it's for the best.
We'll make a winning team -- and sod the rest!

Henry: Gosh, Eleanor! You're just the girl for me!
We'll found a glori'us empire, just you see!

(Henry and Eleanor exit, arm in arm).

Edmund: They'll have some sons and daughters, I should say –
And triumph over Louis on the way.

Since Eleanor's so wise and Henry's strong
Their winning partnership cannot go wrong.

Act 3 – approximately 1170 to 1175.

(Enter Henry and Eleanor, arm in arm, with Edmund and the English knights in attendance).

Eleanor: I'm glad that Henry's managed to reform
Chaotic England after Stephen's storm.

He's put in place a scheme of Common Law,
So England's courts are fair for evermore.

Henry: I've brought the French and Louis to their knees.
Our Empire runs down to the Pyrenees.

(Henry gets a bit agitated, and raises his voice).

But what a job to keep it all at peace!
It seems my visitations *never* cease.

(Edmund addresses the audience, with one eye on Eleanor)

Edmund: Our Henry's got a temper! Have a care!
When *he* gets angry, *we* all live in fear!

(Henry gets more agitated)

Henry: There's trouble back in England, so they say:
A priest called *Boris Becket's* holding sway.

He thinks he should be free from ev'ry rule
That binds the rest of us, the pompous fool!

His mate, *Archdeacon Mogg*, I cannot bear!
Come, who will rid me of this noisome pair?

English: We'll do it! .... No we won't!

(The English appear to divide into two groups).

Yes, we certainly will! .... No we jolly well won't!
Let's have a vote! ... Oh no, not that again!

(Henry gets even more agitated. He shouts loudly)

Henry: Make up your bloody minds!

(Exit Edmund & English knights, terrified, muttering "Let's have an Election". "No, no, anything but that" etc. etc.).

Eleanor: May I suggest a way to calm them down?
Let's move the capital from London town.

The centre of our Empire's further south.
Bordeaux's a goodly port, a river's mouth.

The weather's sunny and, my dear, the wine!
Sod London! Move! Bordeaux would do just fine!

Henry: A good idea, but now is not the time.
For, first, our sons must toe the fam'ly line.

I have five sons. You'd think that that was good,
But two are not behaving as they should.

(Enter Prince Richard, swaggering, and Prince John, mincing).

Richard: Now here come I, I'm Richard Coeur de Lion,
I am the House of Anjou's greatest scion!

I like to fight and throw my weight around:
I want to go abroad and Empires found!

But Dad won't let me go, which is annoying.
I find his discipline a little cloying.

John: I'm John, I'm darling Mother's pride and joy.
I've always been her fav'rite little boy.

My Dad wants me to take on manly tasks
But I don't want to do the things he asks.

He thinks I should be striding round and fighting
But I've no taste for anything exciting.

Henry: You're bad! A sense of duty do you lack!
You both deserve a really hefty smack!

Eleanor: They're only playing! All they want is land.
Give each a province, then they'll come to hand.

Give John and Richard provinces to rule
And then you'll find they cease to play the fool.

Henry: I surely cannot trust them! ... What a life! *(Shouts loudly)*
I don't believe I even trust my wife!

(Henry storms off in a towering rage)

Eleanor: Let's go, my boys, it's time we took a break.
When Henry's mad, no progress can we make.

(Eleanor puts her arm round Richard and John and they go off together).

Act 4. Approx. 1175 to 1189.

(Enter Edmund).

Edmund: Now things have sadly started to unravel:
Queen Eleanor is not allowed to travel.

She's got to stay in England, on her own,
Whilst Henry rushes grimly up and down

To Aquitaine, to Brittany, and more,
To check compliance with the English law.

Back here, she's wondering about succession
And if her sons can make a good impression.

(Enter Eleanor, in conversation with Richard and John).

Eleanor: Now, both of you may one day rule this land.
So, tell, if you could wave a magic wand,

What would you want to be remembered by?
What would you hope to do before you die?

So, come on Richard, let us hear from you.
What noble deeds would *you* aspire to do?

Richard: I'm good at fighting and I fear no foe.
My knights are keen to follow where I go.

I have a project that is bound to please:
Extend the Anj'vin Empire overseas!

I'd join the next Crusade without delay
And take the Isle of Cyprus on the way.

There's distant lands with useful stuff for free;
Exotic spices – and a herb called *Tea.*

We'd conquer many lands until, you bet,
The Sun would *never* on our Empire set!

Eleanor: For that you'd get a Statue back at home,
But maybe you'd be cursed across the foam?

And all your foreign travel: who would pay?
And who would rule while you were far away?

Now your turn, John. If you were to be King,
What triumphs and achievements would you bring?

John: I've no desire to fight in foreign wars
Or get involved, however just the cause.

If I were King, no duties from the past;
For me, it's England first and Europe last.

Although the English gentry's somewhat lax,
I'd show them who is boss by raising tax.

I'd build myself a palace with the loot.
A plot at Runnymede-on-Thames would suit.

Eleanor: An *English ... Gated ... Palace* is your aim?!!
No place for *you* in hist'ry's Hall of Fame!

Unless you take an international view
Our Empire's end will all be down to you.

So, John and Richard: go and contemplate
How you would deal with Europe's muddled state.

(Richard and John exit, looking thoughtful and slightly chastened by their Mother. Eleanor also looks thoughtful).

I think we need to make a grand alliance
'Twixt England, Anjou and the rest of France.

But Henry and King Louis won't agree.
They're too concerned with local pride, you see.

From active politics I shall retire
To Fontevraud, an Abbey on the Loire.

And there I'll gather all the useful facts
For open borders, common trading pacts.

My vision is to bring the nations peace,
So Franco-English emnity will cease.

(Eleanor exits to the Abbey of Fontevraud).

Edmund: Well, I predict that Henry soon will die.
Then Richard will be King, and sparks will fly!

May Eleanor remain to hold his hand,
For *she's* the guiding conscience of this land.

(Edmund goes out, thoughtfully).

Act 5. Approx. 1189 to 1204.

(Enter Edmund).

Edmund: King Henry died and Richard Lion-heart roared.
He spent his time adventuring abroad.

Now Richard's dead and John has got the throne.
And things are in an awful mess back home.

The Ang'vin Empire's sadly on the wane,
For England's weak and France is set to gain.

King Louis died. Now Philip's King of France.
He's leading English troops a merry dance.

(Enter the English knights staggering backwards, trying to fend off the French knights who enter front-wards, pushing the English. There's lots of fighting).

French kn. Europe belongs to us! ... Get out, you English dogs!
Europe, c'est á nous! Europe, c'est á nous!

English kn. Europe's rubbish! .... Crazy foreigners! Who wants them? We're well out of it. Keep your ruddy garlic!

(Enter Maurice and one French knight who did not enter previously. They carry the body of Eleanor. Behind come the ghosts of Henry and Louis).

Maurice: Attention! Arrete! ..... Fait attention! Silence!

(The English and French knights suddenly stop fighting. All turn in silent horror, to face Eleanor's body and the ghosts. Maurice speaks solemnly, in prose).

Maurice: Queen Eleanor is dead! Alas, ... Queen Eleanor is dead! Both France and England must mourn the passing of this noble lady.

(Eleanor is laid at the front of the stage. All look on her body with genuine grief. The ghosts of Henry & Louis kneel).

Edmund: Alas, here lies a lady kind and wise,
Whose vision touched the European skies.

She sought to calm all nationalistic rage,
And unify the European stage.

(Edmund thoughtfully and slowly speaks these lines, shouting the last line triumphantly).

Some talk of Boris Johnson,
And some of Jeremy,
Of Sturgeon and Jo Swinson,
And such buffoons as these.
But of all our politicians there's none who stand so sure
With a tah rah rah and a tah rah rah,
As the good ***Queen Eleanor***.

(The whole cast now stand and sing ♫ these words to the tune of the British Grenadier).

All: ♫ Some talk of Boris Johnson,
♫ And some of Jeremy,
♫ Of Sturgeon and Jo Swinson,
♫ And such buffoons as these.
♫ But of all our politicians there's none who stand so sure
♫ With a tah rah rah and a tah rah rah,
♫ As the good ***Queen Eleanor***.

End.

A10. The Duke of Bridgewater's Canal.

Cast, in order of appearance.

Francis,	third Duke of Bridgewater.
Elizabeth Gunning,	the Duke's friend
John Gilbert,	the Duke's Agent
James Brindley,	an engineer
The Worsley water-sprite	a mythical nymph.
The poor citizens of Manchester	the Chorus; they could played by children.

The water sprite at Worsley Delf

Bridgewater

The action takes place firstly in a London drawing room and then outside Worsley Hall, Lancashire – to the north of Manchester city centre. The events represented in this play took place between about 1758 and 1765.

(Enter the Duke).

Duke: I'm Francis, Duke of Bridgewater, no less!
Right now my love-life's in a frightful mess.

My dearest Jane and I were to be wed –
But then she chose another man instead.

(The Duke sulks. Enter Elizabeth).

Eliz.: Now here come I, Elizabeth, his friend.
I rather wish his heart to *me* would bend.

He is an orphan and, at twenty-one,
To be a Duke he seems so very young.

The poor boy needs a wife. Oh Francis, see
How you could make a Duchess out of me!

Duke: My good Elizabeth, you do not know
How tired of London's social life I grow!

Though ladies chase me for my noble birth,
I shall not marry till I've proved my worth!

So farewell, London, and your intrigues dire.
I'll go to my estates in Lancashire!

(The Duke exits).

Eliz.: To Lancs? That's north of Watford, so I'm told!
A funny place to search for fame and gold!

The roads up there are bad, the people poor.
The Duke has damned himself for ever more!

(Elizabeth starts to exit, then returns).

But wait! I'll stay and watch what now takes place,
And join you onlookers in time and space.

(Behind her, scenery is re-arranged).

The year is 1758; the scene
Is Worsley Hall, a house which lies between

The rugged hills of Lancs and Cheshire's plain –
A spot which gets an awful lot of rain.

The Duke owns Worsley and, nearby, this hole
Is where his trusty miners dig for coal.

(Elizabeth joins the audience and waits for the action to continue. When the scenery is ready, Gilbert enters).

Gilbert: Now here come I, John Gilbert. I'm the one
That Bridgewater employs to get things done.

I am the Agent of the noble lord.
I tell him what he can, and can't, afford.

(Enter Duke).

Duke: Hello there, Gilbert, manager and mate!
Pray, tell me, how are things on my estate?

Is Worsley worth developing? And how
Can we improve the income here and now?

Gilbert: The only source of profit is the coal,
And to improve the mine should be our goal.

Two problems: first, there's flooding in the mine,
And secondly, the transport's far from fine.

To carry coal by road is much too dear –
Which limits us to selling it quite near.

Bridgewater

Duke: The town of Manchester's but eight miles hence:

(The Duke points in the direction of Manchester)

To sell coals there would make a lot of sense.

Gilbert: Oh no, your Grace, the carters charge so much
Our price would be too high for folk to touch.

(The Chorus of poor citizens of Manchester enter. They remain somewhat in the background, ready to chant at key moments in the ensuing drama).

Chorus: Coal, coal, is what we need
To keep us warm, to cook our feed.
Ten thousand tons we'd burn each year
If only coal were not so dear!

Gilbert: We must find cheaper ways of carrying coal.
Yes, *that* must be our most important goal!

Duke: In France, *canals* are what I've seen them use.
To carry coal, canals are what *we'll* choose.

In France, the goods are 'scent' by Chanel Cinq;
In Lancashire, we'd call it Canal Lank!

Gilbert: To build the first canal we'll need some aid:
A man with 'carnal' knowledge, and a spade!

(Enter Brindley).

Brindley: Now here come I, James Brindley is the name.
A load of carnal knowledge do I claim!

Well, actually I am an engineer
And there's no task or challenge that I fear!

The river Irwell is two miles away
And flows from Manchester down to the sea.

(Brindley points in the direction of the sea).

If your canal from Worsley were to link
With Irwell, then your problem's solved, I think!

Gilbert: The company that owns exclusive right
To Irwell shipping wont, without a fight,

Allow us access to their property.
Your plan is much too alimentary!

Duke: We must be bold! We can't with *rivers* mix!
Come, James, show us some engineering tricks!

Brindley: We'll build an aqueduct at Barton - here-

(Brindley points to Barton)

And come upon yon market from the rear!

(Brindley gesticulates rudely. Squeals from Manchester folk).

The aqueduct will have to be quite high:
A veritable river in the sky.

Chorus: Forty feet high? Forty feet high?
You can't build an aqueduct forty feet high!
The winter is cold - our children will die!
You *must* build an aqueduct forty feet high!

Duke: I like your plan. I have another line:
Could our canal drain water from the mine?

The flooding in this hill is quite severe.
They say a water-sprite is living there!

Gilbert: Why can't our barges travel underground?!
The gain in loading coal would be profound!

Duke: Come, let us start to dig at Worsley Delf.
The money for the work I'll find myself.

Bridgewater

(The three position an (imaginary) aqueduct across the River Irwell).

Our plan requires a Parliament'ry Bill,
As well as lots of money in the till!

(Elizabeth advances from the audience and joins the action. She holds in her hand a Parliamentary Bill).

Eliz.: Well, here's your Bill: we understand the need.
The folk of Manchester hope you succeed!

The news of your erection's everywhere.
I didn't know you had it in you, dear!

Duke: The cost of this has nearly made me broke.
The first canal in England is no joke!

Gilbert: The Grand Unveiling has arrived at last.
The coal will get to market cheap and fast.

Behold! The Worsley Water Sprite appears!
And in her hand a piece of coal she bears!

(Water sprite slides from under a theatrical 'hill' and onto the aqueduct).

Chorus: God bless the Duke! God bless you, Sire!
We've coals a'plenty for our fire!
Because of your canal, your Grace,
Now Manchester can grow apace!

Eliz.: Francis, my hero! You have won your fame!
The *Father of Canals* shall be your name!

(Elizabeth pins a medal on the Duke. Everyone applauds him).

End.

A11. Captain Francis Light *or Far East Suffolk.*

Cast, in order of appearance:

Sultan Muhammad Jiwa,	Sultan of Kedah in Malaya
Martina Rozells,	advisor to the Sultan; later, wife of Light
Francis Light,	a Captain in the East India Company
James Scott,	a free-lance trader
Mei	a Chinese servant-girl
Lord Cornwallis	Governor-General of India and boss of the East India Company.

Ah! A valuable spice with fantastic aroma!

Francis Light

The play takes place in Malaya, between about 1770 and 1794.

(Enter the Sultan).

Sultan: Now here come I, a Sultan of Malaya.
I rule the ancient kingdom based at Keddah.

I own this coast - the famed Malacca Straights.
I'm chief amongst the local potentates!

I trade in nutmegs, opium and rice,
And cloves, and other kinds of costly spice.

Although I'm rich, my wealth could eas'ly fade –
For *pirates* lurk nearby to threaten trade.

(Enter Martina).

Martina: Now here come I, the beautiful Martina.
Amongst the Sultan's friends there is none keener.

My Dad was Portuguese, my Mum Malay.
By skill at languages I earn my pay.

I am the Sultan's foreign trade adviser.
My job's to make him wealthier and wiser.

I'm worried that the pirates will appear
And terminate my lucrative career.

Light: Now here come I, I'm Captain Francis Light.
These tiresome pirates don't give *me* a fright!

My ship has guns enough to guard our trade
And beat off threats of any pirate raid.

I'm in the old East India Comp'ny's pay.
My boss is Lord Cornwallis, in Bombay.

My Company seeks cargoes round these shores,
And that's what brings me to the Sultan's doors.

A pity that he speaks a foreign tongue.
Without some help, I might as well be dumb.

Martina: Well, hello sailor! I'll give you a hand!
For I'm familiar with the Sultan's land.

I speak all sorts of tongues: just watch my lips!
I'd love to give a few linguistic tips.

Light: My goodness, gentle lady, thanks indeed!
You're just the sort of person that I need.

And you can start by teaching me your name –
(For love in any language sounds the same!)

Martina: I have a feeling this is love, all right!
I'll gladly be your mentor, Captain Light.

(They move together, rather cosily).

Sultan: Now *that's* the finest sight I've seen all day:
A European keen to learn Malay!

The Portuguese aren't active anymore.
The French and Dutch are constantly at war.

I wonder if this Englishman's all right?
His Company may help us in our fight.

Martina seems to like him 'cos he's lusty.
I'd rather wait and see if he is trusty.

(Sultan exits, looking worried).

Light: Martina: how about some local tips?
I'm looking for a harbour for my ships.

Uncharted coasts pose problems for the stranger,
Especially when the monsoon storms bring danger.

From Shanghai to the River Ganges Delta,
There's nowhere safe for British ships to shelter.

Francis Light

Martina: The Sultan owns an Island that's quite near.
It's called Penang - the safest anch'rage here.

Penang is uninhabited, they say.
Perhaps we'll take a picnic there one day.

Hang on a moment! What's that frightful row?

(Noises off)

Have pirates come, or is it tourists now?

(Enter Scott, dragging Mei by a rope).

Scott: Now here come I, a tip-top chap called Scott.
One finds this Eastern climate frightf'lly hot.

This thing's my Chinese servant, name of Mei.
I bought her in the market yesterday.

She can't speak English, so one has to shout:
"Keep up, you good-for-nothing lay-about!"

I'm passing through from India to China:
A spot of South Sea cruising - nothing finer!

What ho! Another white man! Who are you?
Befriending natives? That will never do!

Light: Come on, my dear, I think it's time we went.
It's clear that mockery is his intent.

I know James Scott: we both served in the Navy.
He was the cad who always got the gravy.

(Light and Martina exit).

Scott: Ah, I remember! Little Francis Light.
A Suffolk oik! We teased him day and night.

His Dad was quite a Suffolk Gent, they say.
His Mum? A parlour-maid, rolled in the hay!

His home was in a place called Dallinghoo –
I've never heard an odder name, have you?

(Enter Cornwallis)

Cornwallis: Now here come I, the Marquis of Cornwallis,
A soldier known for discipline and polish.

Of India I am the Guv'nor Gen'ral –
A post that's more than merely ceremonial.

Round here I represent King George the Third,
And all the British troops obey my word.

I also run a trading corporation:
A cost-effective source of wealth-creation!

Scott: Ah! Lord Cornwallis! You remember me!
We met at Lady Fortescue's for tea.

Cornwallis: Eh? *Do* I know you? … Can't recall your face.
And Lady Fortescue I cannot place.

But, what with fighting Yanks at Yorktown Heights,
I've had to skip society's delights.

Scott: Your Grace, I don't suppose you've got a post
That earns a fellow money round this coast?

Fact is, I'm rather strapped for cash right now.
I need to get a job, but don't know how.

Cornwallis: Well, maybe you can help me with this prob.
If you prove useful, then you've got a job.

(Cornwallis holds up a letter).

This letter came to me. It's rather funny:
A plan to save the Company much money.

The letter's from a chap called Francis Light.
The idea that he's had could well be right.

He says we need a harbour on this coast –
A kind of victualling-place and trading post,

A refuge from high winds and stormy waters,
A fortress 'gainst the French and all marauders.

Could you investigate this chap's suggestions?
Conduct a peer-review and ask some questions!

Scott: I've met this Light: a silly Suffolk man!
I shouldn't trust his judgement or his plan.

I'll go and carry out your peer-review,
Although there's not much point, I'm telling you.

(Scott exits. Mei looks relieved. She starts flicking a duster in odd corners).

Cornwallis: That fellow's odd: he's left his slave behind!
He's either quite forgetful, or unkind.

And as for Seely Suffolk: Scott's a loss!
For I'm a Suffolk man, and I'm the boss!

(Enter Martina and the Sultan, breathlessly).

Martina: Bad news, your Grace! The French have captured Light!
His ship was sunk after a fearsome fight.

Sultan: If Light is killed, our hopes will all go bust
Since he's the only foreigner we trust.

For Light and I had just worked out a deal
About Penang – which you'll approve, I feel.

For sixty thousand pounds I'd sell Penang
If Light would help me fight the pirate gang.

Cornwallis: I like the deal. It certainly suits me.
In time Penang could be our colony.

I'll make Light Gov'nor, if he isn't dead -
It's clear there's no one else we'd trust instead.

Sultan: So ... all our hopes are pinned on Francis Light.
I really hope he has survived the fight.

(Enter Scott, with a swagger. Mei cowers).

Scott: No luck! Light's dead! He's nothing but a ghost.
As his replacement: can I fill his post?

Mei: Don't trust James Scott! I can no more be silent!
This man's dishonest! He's a petty tyrant.

His forté is corruption and abuse.
He only wants Penang for private use.

Martina: Look! Who is this approaching? Can it be
The man we've all been wanting - 'specially me?!

(Enter Light, with head wound & carrying tattered flag)

Light: I'm Captain Light, reporting back for duty!
I'm sorry that this wound has spoilt my beauty!

I managed to escape the Frenchy's prison.
I reached Penang, and started on my mission.

I've built a strong stockade for all my crew.
I've named it 'Fort Cornwallis', after you!

We've nearly cleared the jungle round the fort,
And next we'll build a warehouse for the port.

When all is done, I'll build myself a home
Called Suffolk House, where we can be alone!

(Embraces Martina)

Cornwallis: Well done, that man! And thanks to all your crew.
I wish the Company had more like you.

Sultan: Let me, as Sultan, make the final speech,
And find some lessons that our play may teach.

Francis Light

This hero's found the bay where he may ride.

(Points to Light)

This girl's content to be his loving bride.

(Points to Martina)

Soon Mei will have some dignity and style,

(Points to Mei)

For Light will found a multi-cultur'l Isle.

These gents will huff and strut about the world

(Points to Scott)

Until their Empire's flag is duly furled.

When that day comes, Penang reverts to me –
My Oriental Pearl in silver sea.

End.

B1. Macbeth.

Cast, in order of appearance.

Compère	introduces each scene
Macbeth	a Scottish chief
Banquo	a rather silent friend of Macbeth
Lady Macbeth	
Macduff	a Scottish chief, loyal to King Duncan
Witch 1	leader of the witches
Witch 2, 3, etc.	some more witches
Highland chief 1	another chief loyal to Duncan
Highland chief 2, 3, etc.	some more chiefs.

The Compère's part can be simplified or dispensed with, if required. In our original production the Compère helped some of the younger actors with their parts.

One pint of Fenny Snake coming up!

Our play is in six Acts:

Act 1: Macbeth's castle in Scotland.
Act 2: The *Three Witches* pub.
Act 3: Macbeth's castle in Scotland.
Act 4: The *Three Witches* pub.
Act 5: Macbeth's castle in Scotland.
Act 6: Burnam Wood, near Dunsinane.

Act 1: Macbeth's castle in Scotland.

(The Compère comes on stage, but soon moves to one side, almost out of sight, when not needed).

Comp: Now here come I, I'm Shakespeare's friendly muse.
I'm here to help the actors with their cues.

Our play's about Macbeth, both good and bad,
And how he's rather weak – but then goes mad!

In Macbeth's castle starts our Scottish play.
So let the fun begin without delay!

(Enter Macbeth, closely followed by Banquo)

Macbeth: Now here come I, Macbeth, a highland thane.
And here's my best mate: Banquo is his name.

We serve King Duncan. We're just back from war.
We're tired, so no more fighting any more.

Oh blast! Here comes my rather bossy wife!
Just when I want to have a quiet life.

I need a drink. Quick, Banquo! Down the pub!
We'll have some beers and then a bit of grub.

(Exit Macbeth and Banquo rapidly. Enter Lady Macbeth)

Lady M: Now here come I, the wife of Chief Macbeth.
My man's a wimp! He worries me to death.

The trouble is, he's rather meek and mild.
He lacks ambition and he drives me wild!

He could become as pow'rful as the King!
But – how to get him going, that's the thing.

Right now he's down the pub, the idle fellow.
Let's put some magic on him whilst he's mellow.

(Lady Macbeth gets out her mobile and dials a number)

Hello? … *Three Witches*? … Are the bar-maids there?
The ones with pointy hats and straggly hair?

(Lady Macbeth listens to her 'phone)

Ah yes, you're there. … Now listen to my plan.
Please put a fighting spell upon my man.

(Lady Macbeth ends the call and puts her mobile away)

Those bar-maids at the pub: they'll spike his drink.
And then Macbeth will toughen up, I think!

(Lady Macbeth exits. After a slight pause, enter Macduff)

Macduff: Now here come I, Macduff, another thane.
I think this talk of fighting is a shame.

Our good King Duncan is a worthy man.
My job is to protect him, if I can.

Lady Macbeth is not a pleasant person.
I better warn the King before things worsen!

I may be gone some time, but never fear! Oh!
I come into the last Act as a … hero!

(Exit Macduff. End of Act 1).

Act 2: The *Three Witches* pub.

(The scene opens with three witches sitting round a Cauldron. The Compère is almost off-stage, barely visible).

Comp: We're in a pub famed for its magic potions.
Now this is where Macbeth has other notions!

Witch 1: Now here we sit, upon the blasted heath,
With pointy hats, and rotten hair and teeth.

(Macbeth and Banquo come in, with beer mugs in their hands).

Macbeth: The old *Three Witches* is my fav'rite bar -
The finest pub in Scotland – near or far.

(The witches sing to the tune of: half a pound of tuppenny rice).

All witches: ♫ Half a pint of Adnams Ale,
♫ Add a plop of dog poo.
♫ Then a smelly fish's tail
♫ All mixed with snail goo.

♫ Mix it up and stir it well
♫ Let it foam and bubble.
♫ Wow! It's got an awful smell!
♫ Macbeth's in trouble!

(The witches fill Macbeth's & Banquo's mugs from a jug full of the mixture).

Macbeth: Ah, thank you, barmaids. Yes, I need some beer.
My nagging wife is making me despair.

(Macbeth takes a long swig from his mug. Banquo leaves his untouched).

This drink works magic! And it's got a sting!
Now, Banquo, I feel mighty as a king!

Let's ask old Duncan if he'll abdicate.
And let me have a turn at being great.

Farewell, barmaids, your mixture I adore.
It gives me strength! I'll soon be back for more!

Come on, old Banquo, to my castle run.
Let's talk to Duncan. Then we'll have some fun!

(Macbeth and Banquo exit gleefully. The witches exit with the jug. End of Act 2).

Act 3: back at Macbeth's castle.

Comp: In Macbeth's castle, Lady M's a plotter.
And this is where her evil plot gets hotter!

(Enter Lady Macbeth)

Lady M: King Duncan and his faithful son and heir,
Wee Malcolm, came this way – and now they're here!

I've asked them both to stay and have some dinner.
I have a cunning plan that seems a winner.

They're resting now and, whilst they're still asleep,
We'll stab them! And they'll die without a peep!

It only needs two stabbings, quick and clean.
Macbeth can take the crown – and I'll be queen!

(Enter Macbeth with a swagger, and Banquo meekly)

Macbeth: We'll not delay. ... I'll talk to Duncan now.
I feel as good as royal, anyhow.

Lady M: That's fine, because I've got a cunning plan
To make you king without delay, my man!

For Duncan and his Malcolm sleep next door
Just tip-toe in and stab them while they snore.

Macbeth: What? Stab them both? I'm not much use at killing.
Get someone else to do it. I'm not willing.

Lady M: Go on, you coward! This will see them dead.
I've got a headache and I'm off to bed.

(Lady Macbeth gives Macbeth a parcel containing a dagger, then she exits. Macbeth unwraps the parcel)

Macbeth: Is this a dagger that's before my eyes?
I grasp it by the handle – is this wise?

Banquo: Let go! I can no longer silence keep!
You mustn't kill the King whilst he's asleep!

Macbeth: Take that, Banquo! You shall not stop me now!
I'm better off without you, anyhow.

(Macbeth stabs Banquo, who falls down dead)

And now I go to do the dreadful deed.
Duncan and Malcolm in their beds shall bleed!

And if the stabbings go without some hitches
I'll go and have a drink at the *Three Witches.*

(Exits, dragging Banquo's body. Screams and groans are heard. End of Act 3).

Act 4: At the *Three Witches.*

(The scene opens with three witches sitting round a Cauldron. The Compère is almost off-stage, barely visible).

Comp: The deed is done! We're down the pub again.
The witches' brew infiltrates Macbeth's brain!

Witch 1: This brew is smelly and it really hums.
But listen! Something wicked this way comes!

(Macbeth enters with his mug, looking glum but with a crown on his head. The witches sing to the tune: 'half a pound of tuppenny rice).

All witches: ♫ Half a pint of Adnams Ale,
♫ Add a plop of dog poo.
♫ Then a smelly fish's tail
♫ All mixed with snail goo.

♫ Mix it up and stir it well
♫ Make it thick and gloopy.
♫ Wow! It's got an awful smell!
♫ Macbeth's gone loopy!

(The witches fill Macbeth's mug from a jug full of the mixture).

Macb: Ah, thank you, Barmaids. Phew! I need some beer.
I've killed the King! But not his son and heir!

I stabbed King Duncan whilst in bed he lay,
But Malcolm woke and quickly ran away.

So, tell me, witches, what is there to do?
Am I the king? Is Malcolm now king too?

Witch 1: Be bloody, bold and resolute till death,
For none of woman born shall harm Macbeth.

Fear not, Macbeth. You never will be slain
Till Birnam Wood shall come to Dunsinane.

Macbeth: Ha Ha! That means I'm invincible! .... Invincible! ...
Ha Ha!

(Macbeth exits with an evil cackle, repeating "Invincible!" End of Act 4).

Act 5: The castle, next morning.

Comp: We're back at Macbeth's castle for a feast.
The highland chiefs aren't happy in the least!

(Enter three Highland Chiefs and Lady Macbeth).

Chief 1: Now here we come, three Highland Chiefs so sure.
We've heard that good King Duncan is no more.

Lady M: That's very true. Macbeth has killed him dead.
His awful deed now fills my heart with dread.

Chief 1: We even hear he bumped off Banquo too.
Macbeth's an evil man. What shall we do?

(Enter Macbeth, growling fiercely. The chiefs bow before him)

Macbeth: I see you chiefs have come to celebrate
Your new and pow'rful king! That's really great!

This crown; it rather suits me, don't you think?
Let's have a feast. ... Wife! Bring on food and drink!

(Lady M quickly fetches some supplies. They prepare to eat)

Chief 1: That crown belongs to Malcolm, Duncan's heir.
You should not wear it! You should take great care.

Macbeth: Stop moaning! I'm invincible, I'm told.
Let's taste this food and drink before its cold.

(They sit down to eat. The three Highland chiefs mumble angrily. Behind them, the ghost of Banquo creeps in unnoticed. Then suddenly Banquo raises his arms and shrieks.)

Banquo: Woo! Boo! .... Shoooooo!

(Lady Macbeth screams and falls down in a faint. The three chiefs hurry out looking worried, followed by Banquo's ghost).

Macbeth: I bet they'll raise an army to dispatch me.
Well, let them try! I'll laugh if they attack me!

For I'm invincible. I'm not insane!
I'm going to a hill called Dunsinane.

The Witches said that that's the place for me
To stop attacks from any enemy.

(Macbeth exits, swaggering and dragging the prostrate Lady Macbeth. End of Act).

Act 6: Birnam Wood, near the hill of Dunsinane.

Comp: It's Birnam Wood. Macduff comes round the bend,
And soon Macbeth will meet a sticky end!

(Enter Macduff and the three Highland Chiefs with drawn swords. They don't notice Macbeth crouched down behind a rock a little distance away).

Macduff: We're close to Dunsinane, where lurks Macbeth.
Let's go and whack him hard for Duncan's death.

Let ev'ry man cut branches for disguise.
Be quiet and give Macbeth a big surprise.

(They gather branches. Macduff leads the highland chiefs off stage, singing a marching song. They will re-appear later. As soon as they've gone, Macbeth gets up from behind his rock and brandishes his sword fiercely).

Macbeth: The witches said I never shall be slain
Till Birnam Wood shall come to Dunsinane.

But what is this? A wood is coming here?
There's lots of soldiers. Each a branch does bear!

They said that none of woman born shall harm me.
I'll never fear Macduff, nor all his army!

(As each highland chief drops his branch and comes up to fight, Macbeth easily cuts him down with one blow of his sword. At last, only Macduff is left).

Ha! Only you are left! Lay on, Macduff,
And damned be him who first cries 'Hold! Enough!'

(Macduff and Macbeth fight. Macduff stabs Macbeth, who falls to the ground, dead. Macduff picks up the crown and holds it high).

Macduff: I'm not of woman born: Caesarean, me!
Macbeth is *not* invincible, you see!

Let Scotland cheer! The evil one is down!
Macbeth's no more and *Malcolm* has the crown.

(Macduff pauses, thinks for a moment, and then says)

This story has a moral, don't you think?
"Beware of Witches who might mix your drink!"

End.

B2. The Tempest

Cast, in order of appearance.

Master	of the ship
Bosun	of the ship
Prospero,	the rightful Duke of Milan.
Miranda,	his daughter
Ariel,	a spirit, Prospero's magic messenger
Caliban,	a monster.
Ferdinand,	son of the King of Naples.
Alonso,	King of Naples.
Antonio (Tony),	brother & usurper of Prospero.
Sebastian,	brother of the King. An evil schemer.
Waves,	played by children under one or two blue sheets.

The Island's mine, at last!

Tempest

Act 1: scene 1 at sea, within sight of the island;
scene 2 on the island at Prospero's cell.
Act 2: another part of the island;
Act 3: back at Prospero's cell.

Act 1, Scene 1:
At sea, close to an island. A storm is raging. We see a ship with just two crew visible (the Master and the Bosun). They are about to be engulfed by the waves. In the background, Prospero and Miranda stand almost out of sight on a headland, looking on. Prospero and Miranda remain silent and are invisible to the Master and the Bosun.

Master: Now here stand I, the Master of this barque.
I'm soaking wet and things are looking stark!

This storm's the fiercest one I've ever known.
I think we're lost. We're very far from home.

We've got some wealthy passengers aboard:
The King, a Prince, a Duke and one young lord.

(Briefly we see a crown thrust above the waves)

They're down below, complaining of the motion,
Afraid to face the danger of this ocean.

Hey, Bosun! Get the crew to brace the yard
And put the tiller over: grip it hard!

Bosun: Unless we go about and bring her round
I fear the ship is lost and we'll be drowned.

The topmast's gone! The rocks are very near.
We'll soon be swamped – and then all's lost, I fear!

Master: We cannot bring her round. The wind's too strong!
We're nearly on the rocks! It won't be long!

(The waves engulf the ship, the Master and the Bosun)

I'm drowning! .... All is lost! ... Farewell my mates!
I sink and leave you to your sep'rate fates.

(Master & Bosun exit, followed by the waves).

Act 1 Scene 2:
On the island, outside Prospero's cave. Prospero and Miranda, who have not actually left the stage, slowly move to the centre.

Prospero: Now here stand I, the Master of this Isle.
Be calm, you waves! You tempest, rest a while.

By magic did I summon you to roar
But now I have some other plans in store.

Today's the special day I've long awaited –
For hitherto my hopes have been frustrated.

Miranda: My name's Miranda; Prospero's my Dad.
He's very sweet, although a trifle mad.

I wonder why he weaves these pow'rful spells?
His purposes to me he never tells.

So, Father dear, I beg of you to say
Why this is what you call a *special* day?

Prospero: Ah well, my dearest child, let me recall
The treacheries that caused our star to fall.

When you were young, we lived in fair Milan,
Where I was Duke and was a wealthy man.

My people loved me; ev'rything was fine. . . er
. . , sublime ... er ... (pauses emotionally)

Miranda: Oh, Father – do you *have* to speak in rhyme?

Prospero: I let my brother manage my estate
And never knew that in his heart was hate.

He stole my lands and told the King some lies.
The King pronounced me bad, my brother wise.

At length he made my brother, Tony, Duke
And all I got was insults and rebuke.

Miranda: How awful! Never have I heard this hist'ry:
Milan and Uncle Tony are a myst'ry.

Prospero: So Tony gained renown and I disgrace.
Then you and I were banished from that place.

They forced us on a ship which, in a while,
Put us ashore to perish on this Isle.

We thought it uninhabited, but found
A Monster and some spirits lurking round.

Miranda: Ah, Caliban the Monster. But you tamed him,
Taught him to talk, to serve us. And you named him.

But as for spirits, these I cannot see.
You say this Isle's enchanted: not for me.

Prospero: You cannot see my special spirit Ariel,
My messenger, my sprite of spells ethereal.

Miranda: Don't talk in riddles, Father! Tell me true.
What's happened to the ship and all its crew?

(Miranda points to the sea, where we last saw the Master and Bosun drowning).

The storm has passed. Did anyone survive?
Did anybody reach our shore alive?

Prospero: A king, two nobles, sailors, and my brother
Survived – each unaware of any other.

The King's Alonso; Ferdinand's his son.
Sebastian's his bro – the evil one!

Miranda: Are these the nobles from Milan who hate you?
The ones that took your Dukedom to frustrate you?

Prospero: Yes! … Now they're lost in fear and trepidation.
They wander round the Isle in isolation.

So rest awhile, Miranda. Close your eyes.
When you awake, you'll have a fine surprise!

(Miranda settles down and goes to sleep. Enter Ariel)

Ariel: Now here come I, the nimble spirit Ariel.
I am my Master's messenger ethereal.

But hold! … I draw the line at speaking verse!
For spirits such as I, there's nothing worse!

Command me, Master!

Prospero: Oh, very well. No verse for you. But tell:
Are all the shipwrecked nobles safe and well?

Ariel: All safe, Master! Not a blemish on their garments. The ship is hidden in a secret bay, the mariners asleep and under hatches. The King's son Ferdinand is wandering by himself, believing that his father is drowned. King Alonso is sitting all alone.

Prospero: Well done, my spirit. Now, do tell me more.
Sebastian and Tony: what's in store?

Ariel: The king's brother Sebastian is scheming with Antonio. They are looking everywhere for the King. They mean to kill him! Then Sebastian will take the throne for himself.

Prospero: Those two are evil men – as is the King.
Just let them be for now, then later bring

Them to my cell. … Now, fetch me Ferdinand.
For him I've something rather special planned!

Ariel: I fly, Master! See me fly!

(Ariel exits speedily)

Prospero: My dear Miranda needs a partner's hand --
Perhaps she'll fall in love with Ferdinand?

Hey, Caliban! ... Ho, slave! Get on your feet.
Come tidy up my cell: we've guests to greet.

(Enter Caliban, grumbling)

Caliban: May toads and beetles plague you! My name's Caliban, by the way.

Prospero: Fetch some logs for the fire, you noisome Monster! Who told you to speak?

Caliban: You taught me language, so I know how to curse! This Island belonged to Sycorax, my Mother, and now it should belong to me!

Prospero: Your mother was an evil witch! Go and fetch some logs, or I'll fill your bones with aches and pains. Away, I say, Away!

(Caliban exits. Enter Ariel (singing?), followed by Ferdinand).

Ariel: Full fathom five thy father lies.
Of his bones are coral made.
Those are pearls that were his eyes;
Nothing of him that doth fade. . . .

Come along, Ferdinand, follow me. Don't fret about your father, the king. Come and meet someone much more interesting!

Prospero: Wake up, Miranda! Come and see who's here.
A nobleman he is, so have no fear.

(Miranda wakes up and looks at Ferdinand with amazement)

Miranda: Who is this divine person? Is he spirit or human? Indeed how noble he looks!

Ferdinand: Who is this goddess? Oh, wond'rous vision, may I get to know you better?

Miranda: As far as I'm concerned, the sooner the better! But you should ask my Dad first.

Prospero: Prince Ferdinand! You're welcome in this place.
I'm sure you'll find Miranda full of grace.

Why don't you get to know my daughter well
By taking time to tidy up my cell?

(Miranda and Ferdinand go out, holding hands).

They seem to be good friends. I have a feeling
I won't need Caliban to do the cleaning!

I think that Monster's run away from me
To other parts. So, let us go and see.

(Prospero and Ariel go out)

Act 2: Another part of the Island.

(Enter Caliban).

Caliban: A thousand curses on my master, Prospero. Why should I fetch wood for him and his oh-so-precious daughter Miranda? They despise me and I despise them! It's all too much for a body. I think I'll lie here a while and have a rest. Why work when you can sleep?

(Caliban settles down and sleeps. Enter Bosun).

Bosun: Phew! I've survived that terrible storm but I seem to be the only person alive on this island. I'm so very tired. I think I'll rest under this heap of woolly skin here.

(Lies head to toe with Caliban; dozes. After a pause, enter Master holding a bottle and clearly a bit tipsy. He sings:

Master: ♫ I shall no more to sea, to sea; here shall I die ashore.
♫ That storm it was enough, enough, and I shall sail no more.

Caliban: What awful singing! Do not torment me, Master!

Master: What's this? Have we a devil here? A monster? A Monster with four legs, I see! Here's a mouth at this end. Drink a little of this, Monster, and may it cure your extra legs!

(The Bosun emerges from under Caliban):

Bosun: Hello, Sir! Is it really you? Are you well?
How did you escape?

Master: Well I never! Hello, Bosun! When the ship foundered, I grabbed hold of a barrel of wine and floated ashore on it. Very good wine there was in that barrel, very good wine indeed and I've now got the barrel well hidden! But tell me, how did you get ashore?

Bosun: I swam like a duck – like a very thirsty duck. Is there wine for me in your barrel?

Caliban: And is there more wine for me, Master? I'll be your servant and teach you all the mysteries of this island if you give me another drink. I'll tell you what: If we do away with Prospero and Miranda and steal their jewels then you can be boss of this Island.

Master: All right, Monster, whatever you say. Lead the way and we'll all get drunk together!

(He sings):

♫ The Bosun, the Monster, the Barrel and me
♫ We're all very safe on the land.
♫ We're none of us going again to sea,
♫ For we've got a big barrel to hand, to hand,
♫ For we've got a big barrel to hand!

(All exit, Caliban leading. Enter Areil).

Ariel: Ha ha! They're heading for a boggy place: that will slow them down! But, wait! Here come the three men of evil! Oh dear. Its open-ey'd conspiracy!

(Enter Alonso, followed at a distance by Sebastian and Antonio who creep along with their swords drawn. Alonso looks sleepy, unaware that he is being followed).

Alonso, Sebastian & Antonio: Mutter, mutter, grrr!, mutter.

(Alonso turns suddenly. Sebastian and Antonio hastily hide their swords and continue to march in file behind Alonso).

Ariel: There goes Alonso, followed by Sebastian and Antonio. I've put a spell on them so that they will march up and down until Prospero is ready to deal with them.

(This parade goes back and forth, still muttering, across the stage three times. Sebastian and Antonio, who are trying to summon up courage to stab Alonso in the back, continue to follow, muttering softly. Then all three exit, still in a file).

Ariel: Prospero's plans are working well. Soon everyone will be assembled and then we'll have the grand finale. If Prospero triumphs, then he's promised to set me free – free as a spirit should be!

(Exit Ariel, joyously)

Act 3: back at Prospero's cell.

(Enter Prospero and Ariel).

Prospero: Well done, my lively Spirit! Things progress!
I feel this day will bring us much success.

If all goes well, then, just as we agreed,
I'll scrap my magic book and see you freed!

Now, spirit, fetch the evil men along.
Let's see if they admit to doing wrong.

Ariel: Yes, Master, they're close by! Come along, you three!
Line up! Come and hear your fate.

(Enter Alonso, Sebastian and Antonio, looking fearful. They stand in a row with bowed heads).

Prospero: Most cruelly did you, O King, abuse us.
Sebastian, you shamefully misused us.

Antonio, you greedy little thief
You took my Dukedom, causing us much grief.

What dreadful crimes! They certainly appal.
But ... I forgive! Yes, I forgive you all!

Alonso, Sebastian & Antonio: Phew! ... Mercy on us! Mercy on us!

Prospero: Quite soon I shall be Duke again, you know.

Alonso, Sebastian & Antonio: Yes, of course, absolutely your Grace!
Mercy on us! Mercy on us!

Prospero: And then it's to Milan and home we go.

But first, Alonso, here's a big surprise:
Two love-birds, hand in hand, before your eyes!

(Enter Miranda and Ferdinand, hand in hand).

Alonso: What a miracle! Can this be my son, saved from the tempest? And who is this gorgeous maiden by his side?

Prospero: This is indeed your son and this my daughter.
It seems that Ferdinand some joy has brought her.

If they're in love – which is the case, I guess,
Well then, I wish them ev'ry happiness.

Ferdinand: Miranda, let me introduce my father King Alonso, his brother Sebastian and your uncle Antonio.

(These three bow graciously)

Ferdinand: I see that Antonio and Sebastian look very ashamed of themselves so let's hope that we can all be friends.

Miranda: I've never seen such a gathering of nobles. O Brave New World, that has such people in it!

Alonso: It's clear, Miranda, that you love my son Ferdinand and I approve his choice. So, Miranda, you have my blessing! If we get back to Milan safely then I'll pay for a fine wedding.

Prospero: Amen to that! Now, Ariel my friend,
Bring on the clowns and let us make an end.

Ariel: Caliban and the sailors are close by, Master. Come along, you three boozers! Look lively! Look lively!

(Enter Caliban, the Master and the Bosun, swaying drunkenly)

Prospero: Ho, my fine fellows! What have you to say for yourselves?

Bosun: We've been in such a pickle, sir!

Master: We've found our ship, your Grace. She's bravely rigged and ready to put to sea again. The crew are all fit and well. When would you like to return to Milan?

Prospero: All in good time, all in good time.

Caliban: Oh, Master, oh my head! What a thrice-double ass I was to take up with these mariners. For sure, I'll never drink wine again! I'll be content to serve you peaceably in future, if you let me.

Prospero: Our revels soon are ending on these shores.
Then, Caliban, this island will be yours.

Forget what's gone and do not be afraid,
For we're the stuff of which your dreams are made

And now, my Ariel, my little chick,
Be free! No tears, just fly away – and quick!

(Ariel dances round everyone)

Ariel: I fly! See, nobles, how I fly!
Where the bee sucks, there suck I;
In a cowslip's bell I lie;
There I couch when owls do cry.
On the bat's back I do fly.

Merrily, merrily shall I live now
Under the blossom that hangs on the bough.

(Ariel exits joyfully).

Prospero: Now my charms are all o'erthrown,
And what strength I have's mine own.
Now I have my Dukedom got
And forgave this awful lot.
Come, oh waves, and spread your foam
Take us safely to our home.

(the waves come in with their blue sheets and wrap up all the cast except for Prospero and Caliban. All except for Prospero and Caliban exit by degrees with the waves).

Prospero: Farewell, all! Our revels cease!
Let us leave this Isle in peace.

(Prospero exits, rather pompously)

Caliban: Go, bunch of toffs! Now *I* can speak in rhyme!
At last they've gone ... and all this Island's mine!

End.

B3. Omlet.

Cast, in order of appearance.

Horatio	
Ghost	of Hamlet's father, the old King. The ghost is invisible to all but Hamlet.
Hamlet	
King,	aka Wicked Uncle Claude
Queen,	Hamlet's Mum Gertie, now married to Claude
Polonius,	the Lord Chamberlain
Laertes,	son of Polonius
Ophelia,	daughter of Polonius and Hamlet's sweetheart.

Props to include two swords, each distinct; one cup of poison; one letter; one dagger.

The end – or is it?

Omlet

Act 1: On the castle walls
Act 2: The royal chamber in the castle
Act 3: On the castle walls
Act 4: The royal chamber in the castle.

Act 1. On the castle walls.

(Enter Horatio)

Horatio: Now here come I, Horat'io, Hamlet's mate.
He needs a friend: he's in a frightful state.

He mooches round and round the castle wall –
Refuses to be comforted at all.

For Hamlet's Dad was killed in tragic circs.
It's said his father's ghost still round us lurks.

(Enter Ghost, who is invisible to all but Hamlet)

He thinks his Dad was murderously gored
By order of his wicked Uncle Claude.

(Enter Hamlet, who pushes the Ghost to one side)

Hamlet: Now here come I, I'm Hamlet, Danish Prince.
Of father's ghost you might have caught a glimpse.

(Hamlet points his sword at the Ghost. Ghost exits).

That ghost won't rest until this trusty sword
Has put an end to wicked Uncle Claude!

Horatio: Cheer up, old mate! I think you'll shortly find
The ghost is but a figment of your mind.

(Ghost comes slowly in again, unnoticed)

For none but you can see this apparition.
So, let it rest, or risk the King's derision.

Let's leave this doleful place and take a break.
Perhaps Ophel'ia's walking by the lake?

Hamlet: Ophel-i-a! She's nothing more to me.
She was my girl, but now it's not to be.

I cannot be distracted from my task.
Revenge for father's death is all I ask!

Let's go and see my Mum and Uncle Claude,
And hear what evil schemes they plan abroad.

(They both exit, followed by Ghost)

Act 2. The royal chamber in the castle.

(Enter the King (aka Uncle Claude), Queen Gertie, Polonius the Lord Chancellor and Laertes his son)

King: What's up, my dear? You're looking rather queer.
We're married now. There's nothing you should fear.

The old King, Hamlet's Dad, is truly dead.
He's six feet under and I'm King instead.

Queen: The trouble's Hamlet, who is still my son.
He wanders round, upsetting everyone.

He's grieving, and he thinks you killed his Dad.
The thought of murder's driving him quite mad.

We've got to calm him. Otherwise, you see,
He'll take revenge upon both you and me.

King: What nonsense! Hamlet's just a wayward lad.
He cannot harm us, even if he's mad!

Polonius: My Lord, may I suggest an easy plan
To solve the problem of this tiresome man?

Arrange that Hamlet takes a little trip
To England. Say that you'll provide the ship.

And tell him that it's nothing but a cruise,
Complete with friends and plenty of free booze.

King: A good idea! A cruise we can devise
With Rosencrantz and Guildenstern, my spies!

They're cruel, and on them we can depend
To see that Hamlet meets a sticky end!

(Polonius starts to scribble a note of the arrangements)

Polonius: Laertes! Take this note that I'll devise
To Rosencrantz and Guildenstern, our spies.

And tell them, from the King, they mustn't fail
To take young Hamlet for a … stormy… sail.

(Laertes nods agreement & exits, carrying the note).

Queen: But can we trust Laertes with this task?
Conveying secret notes is much to ask.

Polonius: Laertes envies Hamlet, never fear.
If Hamlet drowns, my son won't shed a tear.

Besides, he disapproves of Hamlet's shine
For sweet Ophel-i-a, dear daughter mine.

(Hamlet is heard shouting, off-stage)

King: Enough! I hear him come! Let's leave the room.
It's best if Gertie talks to him alone.

Polonious: I'll hide behind the arras with my sword.
If Hamlet threatens you, just say the word.

(King Claude exits. Polonius hides behind arras. Enter Hamlet in a rage).

Hamlet: You traitor, Mother! You are really bad!
You've married Claude, the man who murdered Dad!

The pair of you deserve a dreadful fate.
There's something rotten in old Denmark's State.

Queen: What? Did your uncle really kill his brother?
I knew it not. I thought it was another.

But don't get cross. You've made a great mistake
If you intend the power of Claude to break.

(Polonius sneezes loudly behind the arras).

Hamlet: Hush! What's that noise? I think I smell a rat!
Behind the arras! ..... Ho!

(Hamlet stabs wildly at the arras. Polonius yells).

..... Take that! And that!

(Polonius rolls into view, very dead).

Hamlet: Er ... Whoops! .... Polonius! ... I wonder why
You spy on us? You sure deserved to die!

Enough of all this subterfuge and stink!
I need to cool my head and have a think.

(Hamlet storms out)

Queen: Now murder, mostly foul, is in the air!
The King must finish Hamlet, that is clear.

(Exit Queen).

Act 3. On the castle wall.

(Enter Hamlet and ghost. Hamlet holds a dagger).

Ghost: Now just for once, do try to speak in prose!
Your rhyming's really getting up my nose!

(Hamlet sighs deeply. He talks at the ghost, who merely nods occasionally, wandering around aimlessly but saying nothing).

Hamlet: To be, or not to be: that is the question:
Whether 'tis nobler in the mind to suffer
The slings and arrows of outrageous fortune,
Or to take arms against a sea of troubles,
And by opposing end them? To die: to sleep;

(Hamlet turns the dagger on himself and it looks for a ghastly second that he's going to stab himself).

No more; and, by a sleep to say we end
The heart-ache and the thousand natural shocks
That flesh is heir to, 'tis a consummation
Devoutly to be wish'd. To die, to sleep;
To sleep: perchance to dream: ay, there's the rub;
For in that sleep of death what dreams may come
When we have shuffled off this mortal coil,
Must give us pause. ...

(Ghost exits. Ophelia enters slowly, mournfully. Hamlet ignores her in silence).

Ophelia: Now here come I, Ophel'ia, Hamlet's dove.
I've heard such dreadful things about my love.

He hasn't talked to me for sev'ral days.
I hope it's not the parting of the ways.

Dear Hamlet! Speak to me! I feel so bad.
I cannot bear to see you look so sad.

Omlet

Hamlet: I never gave you aught....
It were better my mother had not borne me!
..... Get thee to a nunnery!

(Ophelia falls to her knees, imploringly)

I am but mad north-north-west;
When the wind is southerly, I know a hawk from a handsaw. .... Get thee to a nunnery!

(Hamlet exits slowly, looking grim. Ophelia gets up, groaning).

Ophelia: O! What a noble mind is here o'erthrown:
The courtier's, soldier's, scholar's, eye and tongue.

This is the end. And more I cannot take.
I'll go and throw myself into the lake.

(Exits, distraught, ignoring the incoming Horatio. Horatio enters, looking frantic)

Horatio: What's up with her? ... And why's she looking flat?
Have she and Hamlet had a little spat?

And where is Hamlet? I've important news.
There's danger coming and I need his views.

The King's arranged a special fencing duel
Twixt Hamlet and Laertes, that young fool.

He says it's just a bit of harmless sport
But I suspect it's nothing of the sort.

For Claude's a ruthless schemer. And it's said
He'll fix the fight so Hamlet ends up dead!

Foul treachery's afoot. That much is clear.
So Hamlet needs to take especial care.

(Horatio turns to go, but bumps into Hamlet & turns back. Hamlet enters, clutching a note).

Hamlet: I heard your warning of the coming fight.
For this relief much thanks, but I'm all right.

What's more, I found this curious little note
About a plan to kill me in a boat.

Their booze-cruise scheme, thank God, is put to bed
For Rosencrantz and Guildenstern are dead!

And now, revenge for Father must be won!
So let us get this fencing duel done.

(Exit Horatio and Hamlet).

Act 4. The royal chamber in the castle.

(Enter King, Queen, Laertes. King carries a large cup of poison. Laertes carries two swords).

King: Now careful, all. Remember what we planned.
This flask of poison, keep it close to hand.

(King gives cup of poison to Queen).

Laertes, dip one sword into the flask.
Make Hamlet take the other, that's your task.

(Laertes dips the tip of one sword and keeps this one close to himself. The other he holds ready to give to Hamlet).

One scratch and Hamlet's dead! Make sure you hit,
And then the match is won and you can quit.

(Enter Horatio and Hamlet. Hamlet confronts the King).

Hamlet: Ho! King of shreds and patches! Where's the catch?
What tricks are hidden in this fencing match?

King: It's nothing but a game. Here, take a sword.
Just play for points, that's all. You have my word.

(Laertes gives Hamlet one sword, keeping the poisoned one for himself. They begin to fence).

Laertes: On guard! ... Let's see the way you strut your stuff!
Of all your crazy talk we've heard enough!

Hamlet: Well, don't you fret! I'll show you ev'rything!

(Laertes' sword nicks Hamlet's arm but the sword falls to the floor. Hamlet also lets his sword fall, as he clutches his arm).

Ouch! Just a scratch - but now it starts to sting!

King: A hit, a very palpy hit! All right,
Pick up your swords and get on with the fight.

(They pick up the wrong swords, and continue to fence).

King: You've got that wrong! The poisoned sword's changed side!
Take care, Laertes, lest he nick your hide!

Hamlet: I see your cowardly plan and murd'rous trick!
For that, I'll give your arm a deadly prick!

(Hamlet stabs Laertes in the arm. Both Hamlet and Laertes begin to stagger, as the poison starts to flow through their veins. Laertes falls. Hamlet suddenly swings round and takes the King by surprise).

And you, foul Uncle, now your life shall end!
And thus my noble father is avenged!

(Hamlet stabs the King, who falls down dead upon Laertes. Hamlet continues to stagger in mortal pain).

Queen: What's happened now? Can all three men be dying?
And what becomes of me? There's no use crying,

I might as well be dead! Come, bitter drink!

(Queen drinks of the poisoned cup).

Now quench my flame, as down in death I sink.

(Queen falls down dead on the King and Laertes).

Hamlet: Horatio! My life you cannot save:
I go to seek Ophel'ia in her grave.

(Hamlet staggers, then falls to his knees, head bowed).

Horatio: Now cracks a noble heart. Good night, Prince best,
And flights of angels sing thee to thy rest!

(Hamlet looks up, then stands up indignantly. Horatio looks aghast).

Hamlet: Now wait! ... Alas, poor Yorick: where is he?
This play is incomplete, it seems to me!

(The Queen gets up, also indignantly)

Queen: And what about the omelette? Where's the joke?
A morbid play's an egg without a yolk!

(The King gets up, also indignantly)

King: I thought I'd had my bacon; I was wrong!
I'll stay until my Egg-sit comes along.

(Laertes gets up, also very indignant)

Laertes: I thought I'd had my chips and was a duffer.
Now give me mushroom omelette for my supper!

(Enter Polonius, closely followed by Ophelia and the Ghost).

Polonius: Is this a party? Can we join the fun?
For being dead's no joy for anyone.

Ophelia: That lake was far too cold for skinny dipping.
Ophel'ia's spoken part is hardly gripping.

And Hamlet's part is totally confusing!
His monologues are dense and not amusing.

Ghost: Don't worry. I will have a quiet word.
Henceforth, no complex speeches will be heard.

(Ophelia breaks into prose, in exasperation).

Ophelia: Thank goodness for that!
Horatio! You're the only sensible person round here.
What on earth do we do now?
How can we end the play on a high moral note?
Please, please: let us all at least exit in a dignified manner!

Horatio: A cheesy ending I have now invented:
The poison's not as strong as was intended.

It knocked them out a while, but did not kill.
They woke, shook hands, said sorry with a will.

(King, Queen, Laertes and Hamlet shake hands all round).

Claude abdicated and became a monk.
Laertes lost his nerve and did a bunk.

(Exit King, Queen, Polonius, Laertes and Ghost, each bowing to the audience as they go).

The Queen became a nun and took up knitting.
And Hamlet became King, entirely fitting.

Ophel'ia married Hamlet, as we hoped.
And with affairs of state he nobly coped.

(Hamlet and Ophelia hug each other).

If Omelette is a metaphor for life,
Then Hamlet is the broken egg of strife.

(Horatio bows extravagantly towards Hamlet and encourages the audience to applaud Hamlet & Ophelia).

End.

B4. Midsummer revels *or Mrs Shakespeare's Dream.*

Cast, in order of appearance.

Anne Shakespeare	also plays the Lion in Act 2
Mistress Quickly,	bar-maid at the Mermaid; also Thisbe
Sir Francis Bacon	philosopher and statesman; also the Wall
Richard Burbage,	famous actor; also the Prologue
Nick Bottome,	a would-be actor; also Pyramus
William Shakespeare	also Moonshine

That was certainly worth £20

Midsummer

The action takes place at The Mermaid Inn, London, in about 1600. There are two Acts.

Act 1.

It is late evening. The audience will soon be spilling out of the near-by Globe Theatre, at which Shakespeare's 'A Midsummer Night's Dream' is playing. In the Mermaid, Bacon is seated, drinking. Mistress Quickly is behind the bar.

Enter Anne.

Anne: Now here come I, Anne Shakespeare, William's wife.
Just now I'm not exactly pleased with life.

I never know from one day to the next
If he'll be home or not – I'm really vexed!

Take my advice and never trust a bard,
For life with Will is nothing if not hard!

He stays out nightly, drinking with his mates
And never leaves me money for the rates.

If anybody sees that man of mine,
Then tell him that he's gone too far, this time!

(Anne glares round the pub menacingly).

Quick: Now here be I, the bar-maid of this place.
I've lovely legs, not just a pretty face!

Men call me Mistress Quickly, 'cos I'm speedy
At filling up their pints when they feel needy.

Why, even Shakespeare says that I inspire him -
And I admit that, sometimes, I desire him.

Our Will and all his friends should soon be here,
For this is where the actors come for beer.

Anne: Well, when they come, there's things I want to know.
If they're so good, why don't their profits grow?

If Will were prudent, he would *publish* plays,
And save the profits for the rainy days.

Will's always scribbling bits of flow'ry verse
And yet he seems to have an empty purse.

If only he would *publish* what he writes,
His name would soon be up in brilliant lights.

Bac: Now here sit I, my name's Sir Francis Bacon.
Your views on drama are, I fear, mistaken!

I know a thing or two about the Arts,
And Shakespeare's plays aren't worth a bunch of farts.

He has no proper sense of history.
He mixes up the facts with fantasy.

His latest play's the biggest mess you've seen:
There's Ancient Athens, and ... a Fairy Queen!

Among my friends who matter at the Court,
I fear your Shakespeare's writings count for naught.

Quick: If Shakespeare's plays are intellectual trash,
How come the theatre's raking in the cash?

The Globe, just down the road, is always full,
So I believe you talk a lot of bull.

Anne: There's precious little cash that comes *my* way:
They all forget that *I've* got bills to pay!

(Enter Burbage and Bottome. Burbage carries several props, including a small sword and a cloak, props from that evening's play at the Globe).

Burb: Now here come I, an actor from The Globe.
I'm Richard Burbage; here's my sword and robe.

I'm Shakespeare's friend. He'll soon be coming here,
So, Mistress Quickly: ready with the beer!

Bott: Now here come I, my name is Nick Bottome:
Pronounce it so it rhymes with Ancient Rome!

I've just been watching Shakespeare's latest play.
I'd like to be an actor *too*, one day.

Come, Mr Burbage, let me buy the booze,
Then tell me what you know of Shakespeare's muse.

Could I become an actor, paint my face,
And dress up bright and gay, and pose with grace?

(Bottome strikes an exaggerated pose and flourishes a limp- wristed arm towards an imagined adoring public).

I'd like to join your company right now.
Give me a role, and let me take a bow!

Burb: You'll have to ask Will Shakespeare. He's the boss –
(Though could he magic glitter out of dross?)

Bacon: If Shakespeare gives Bottome an acting part,
He has no feeling for dramatic art.

Anne: He'll have a feeling in his head, for sure,
As soon as William comes in through that door!

(Anne seizes Burbage's sword and hides (or perhaps crouches) behind Bottome. Enter Will Shakespeare. He fails to notice Anne, his wife).

Will: Now here come I, a man of words and notions.
Let me enthral you with my verbal potions.

I'm William Shakespeare, as you might have guessed.
And I could certainly do with a drink.
Oh ... that doesn't rhyme! ... Well, never mind!

Let's press on.

Good ev'ning all! What ho, my Mistress Quickly!
Tonight I'm in the mood for slap and tickly!

(Will advances, grinning, towards Quickly. He still does not notice Anne. After a pause, Anne springs out brandishing the sword).

Anne: Oi! Not so fast, you good-for-nothing worm!
I'm in the mood to slap you till you squirm!

Will: Eek! Anne, my love! How *nice* to see you here!
Put down that sword and come and have a beer.

Anne: Forget the beer! Now, what about some cash?
Pay up, or else I'll give you such a bash!

(Anne takes a wild swing at Will. Mistress Quickly dashes forwards to restrain her. Will backs away. Burbage takes the sword).

Quick: Enough of that, Anne! Let the man explain.
Let's see his purse, before you give him pain.

Will: Right now, my dear, I'm rather short of cash;
But we can raise some money in a flash.

There's six of us: ... we'll do a little play
And busk for ready money right away.

Bac: Hold hard! I hope it's never your intention
To make *me* play a part in your invention?

Will: Oh, come! It's all good humour. Where's the rub?
We often put on sketches in the pub.

Quick: That's right: These people look a likely crew.
You'd love to see some theatre, wouldn't you?

(Quickly addresses the audience, as if they are drinkers at the Mermaid. The audience, having been primed, agree).

Bac: I won't take part in any trite charade –
Not even if it's written by a bard.

Will: Not even if it's one of Ovid's tales?
Like *Pyramus and Thisbe*? Never fails!

(Will produces a bundle of five scripts from his pocket).

Bac: Ah, *Pyramus and Thisbe*: that's all right.
I'll take a part – but only for tonight.

I'll wager, though, that with this classic theme,
Inside this pub you cannot raise a bean.

Will: Then let us bet: If people find it fun
And pay good money, then let's say I've won.

And if they laugh, you pay me twenty quid,
And if they don't, then I'll pay you instead.

Bac: All right. And I'm so sure I'll win the day
That I'll be Pyramus within your play.

Will: No! I'll decide. A part for you I'll choose
That suits your lofty philosophic views.

Your mighty intellect confronts us all;
You'll definitely have to play the *Wall*.

(Will gives Bacon a script).

And you, my love, who rules with rod of iron.
Can play the fiercest part, of course – the Lion.

(Will gives Anne a script).

And what's the role I have for Mistress Quickly?
Why, surely she should play the part of Thisbe.

(Will gives Quickly a script).

Bur: Now here's a chap who wants a dashing part:
Let him have Pyramus to try his art.

(Burbage points to Bottome, who looks eager. Will gives Bottome a script. Burbage gives Bottome the sword and cloak).

Bott.: Oh, goody! Here's my chance to put on make-up!
I'll give the drama critics such a shake-up!

Bur.: Give me the Prologue: that's the part I know.
I'll introduce the cast and start the show.

(Will gives Burbage a script, who then turns to Will).

And you, who are the highlight of the age,
Can shed your silver Moonshine on our stage.

Come on, Sir Francis! Try to raise a smile.
Our little play is *classical* in style.

(Burbage puts an arm round a doubtful Bacon & turns to the audience).

We won't be long: we've got some props to fetch
And then we'll entertain you with our sketch.

(Burbage and Bacon exit).

Bott.: Come, Mistress Thisbe, my new turtle-dove:
Let Pyramus prepare you for his love!

(Bottome puts his arm round a rather alarmed Mistress Quickly and they both exit)

Anne: I don't know what they think they're going to do:
As actors, they're a pretty motley crew.

Will: There's hidden talent each of them can bring,
And, as I always say, "The play's the thing".

Anne: Well, even if the actors cut a dash,
Your play is nothing if it brings no cash.

Will: No worries there! Before the night is done
My bet, and twenty quid, will both be won!

(Will turns to address the audience).

So, audience, be patient for a while,
And we'll return with magic to beguile.

(Will and Anne exit. There is a short interval during which the cast prepare themselves for the play 'Pyramus and Thisbe').

Act 2, The Mermaid Inn, sometime later the same evening.

(Enter Burbage, as the Prologue)

Bur: Here begins the most lamentable comedy, and most cruel death of Pyramus and Thisbe.

(Burbage pauses, bows, and continues).

If we offend, it is with our good will.
That you should think, we come not to offend,
But with good will. To show our simple skill,
That is the true beginning of our end.

(As he reads, Burbage becomes more and more doubtful that he has got the right script. It is not at all the Prologue that he was expecting).

Consider that we come but in despite.
We do not come as minding to content you,
Our true intent is. All for your delight,
We are not here. That you should here repent you.

(Finally, he can contain himself no longer. He spits out the following couplet in an exaggerated stage whisper to the others, who are waiting off stage).

Ye Gods! Whoever wrote this tangled verse?
I think Will's poking fun at us – or worse!

(Burbage just about recovers his composure and continues with the Prologue).

The actors are at hand; and, by their show,
You shall know all that you are like to know.

(All the rest of the cast enter. Bacon (dressed as Wall) is in the lead, closely followed by Anne (dressed as Lion) and the others. Bacon is muttering to himself as he enters).

Bac.: Good grief! The Prologue's making little sense.
I can't believe I'm part of this pretence.

Anne: Hush! Hush! It's not your turn, you silly Wall!
Keep silent, or you'll spoil it for us all.

(The cast line up to be introduced by Burbage. Each one bows as he/she is mentioned).

Bur.: Gentles, perchance you wonder at this show;
But wonder on, till truth make all things plain.
This man is *Pyramus*, if you would know;
This beauteous lady *Thisbe* is, certain.

This man, with lime and rough-cast, doth present
Wall, that vile Wall, which did these lovers sunder;
And through Wall's chink, poor souls, they are content
To whisper, at the which let no man wonder.

This man, with lanthorn, dog, and bush of thorn,
Presenteth *Moonshine*; for, if you will know,
By moonshine did these lovers think no scorn
To meet at Ninus' tomb, there, there to woo.

This grisly beast, which *Lion* hight by name,
The trusty Thisbe, coming first by night,
Did scare away, or rather did affright;

And, as she fled, her mantle she did fall,
Which Lion vile with bloody mouth did stain.
Anon comes Pyramus, sweet youth and tall,
And finds his trusty Thisbe's mantle slain:

Whereat, with blade, with bloody blameful blade,
He bravely broach'd his boiling bloody breast;
And Thisbe, tarrying in mulberry shade,
His dagger drew, and died. For all the rest,

Let Lion, Moonshine, Wall, and lovers twain,
At large discourse, while here they do remain.

(All exit, except Bacon (the Wall)).

Bac: In this same interlude it doth befall
That I, Sir Francis Bacon, am a wall.

And such a wall, as I would have you think,
That had in it a crannied hole, or chink,

(Holds up two fingers, as if they were a chink)

Through which the lovers, Pyramus and Thisbe,
Did whisper often very secretly.

This loam, this rough-cast, and this stone doth show
That I am that same wall; the truth is so.

(Holds up two fingers again, with emphasis).

And this the cranny is, right and sinister,
Through which the fearful lovers are to whisper.

(Enter Bottome (as Pyramus)).

Bott: O grim-look'd night! Oh night with hue so black!
O night, which ever art when day is not!
O night! O night! Alack, alack, alack!
I fear my Thisbe's promise is forgot.

And thou, O wall, O sweet, O lovely wall!
That stand'st between her father's ground and mine;
Thou wall, O wall! O sweet and lovely wall!
Show me thy chink to blink through with mine eyne.

(Bacon (Wall) holds up two fingers again).

Thanks, courteous wall: Jove shield thee well for this!
But what see I? No Thisbe do I see.
O wicked wall! Through whom I see no bliss;
Curs'd be thy stones for thus deceiving me!

(Enter Mistress Quickly (Thisbe)).

Quick: O wall! Full often hast thou heard my moans,
For parting my fair Pyramus and me:
My cherry lips have often kiss'd thy stones,
Thy stones with lime and hair knit up in thee.

Bott: I see a voice: now will I to the chink,
To spy an I can hear my Thisbe's face.

Thisbe! .....

Quick: My love! ... Thou art my love, I think.

Bott: Think what thou wilt, I am thy lover's grace;
And, like Limander, am I trusty still.

Quick: And I like Helen, till the Fates me kill.

Bott: Not Shafalus to Procrus was so true.

Quick: As Shafalus to Procrus, I to you.

Bott: O! Kiss me through the hole of this vile wall.

Quick: I kiss the wall's hole, not your lips at all.

Bott: Wilt thou at Ninny's tomb meet me straightway?

Quick: 'Tide life, 'tide death, I come without delay.

(Exit Bottom and Quickly).

Bac: Thus have I, Wall, my part discharged so;
And, being done, thus Wall away doth go.

(Exit Bacon (Wall). Enter Anne (Lion) and Will (Moonshine)).

Anne: You, ladies, you, whose gentle hearts do fear
The smallest monstrous mouse that creeps on floor,
May now perchance both quake and tremble here,
When lion rough in wildest rage doth roar.

Then know that I, old Mrs Shakespeare, am
A lion-fell, nor else no lion's dam:

For, if I should as lion come in strife,
Into this place, 'twere pity on my life.

Will: This lanthorn doth the horned moon present;
Myself the man i' the moon do seem to be.

(Enter Quickly (Thisbe)).

Quick: This is old Ninny's tomb. Where is my love?

Anne: Rroarr! Rroarr! Rrroarrr!

(Exit Quickly (Thisbe). She drops her mantle in terror and runs away. Anne (Lion) then tears at the mantle with her teeth, and exits leaving the mantle behind).

(Enter Bottome (Pyramus)).

Bott: Sweet moon, I thank thee for thy sunny beams;
I thank thee, moon, for shining now so bright,
For, by thy gracious, golden, glittering streams,
I trust to taste of truest Thisbe's sight.

But stay, O spite!
But mark, poor knight,
What dreadful dole is here!
Eyes, do you see?
How can it be?
O dainty duck! O dear!

Thy mantle good,
What! Stained with blood!
Approach, ye Furies fell!
O fates, come, come,
Cut thread and thrum;
Quail, crush, conclude, and quell!

O! Wherefore, Nature, didst thou lions frame?
Since lion vile hath here deflower'd my dear?
Which is – no, no – which was the fairest dame
That liv'd, that lov'd, that lik'd, that look'd with cheer.

Come, tears, confound;
Out, sword, and wound
The pap of Pyramus:
Ay, that left pap,
Where heart doth hop:
Thus die I, thus, thus, thus.

(Bottome (Pyramus) stabs himself).

Now am I dead,
Now am I fled;
My soul is in the sky:
Tongue, lose thy light!
Moon, take thy flight!

(Exit Will (Moonshine)).

Now die, die, die, die, die.

(Bottome (Pyramus) dies a lingering death).

(Enter Quickly (Thisbe)).

Quick: Asleep, my love?
What, dead, my dove?
O Pyramus, arise!
Speak, speak! Quite dumb?
Dead, dead! A tomb
Must cover thy sweet eyes.

These lily lips,
This cherry nose,
These yellow cowslip cheeks,
Are gone, are gone:
Lovers, make moan!
His eyes were green as leeks.

O, Sisters Three,
Come, come to me,
With hands as pale as milk;
Lay them in gore,
Since you have shore
With shears his thread of silk.

Tongue, not a word:
Come, trusty sword:
Come, blade, my breast imbrue:

(Stabs herself)

And farewell, friends;
Thus Thisbe ends:
Adieu, adieu, adieu.

(She dies, falling in a heap across Pyramus. The lights dim).

(After a pause, Will, Anne, Bacon and Burbage enter slowly and sadly, in that order, to mourn the dead lovers).

(Burbage carries a hat which he later hands to Quickly for the 'collection').

Will: Now here comes Moonshine, to illume the dead.

Anne: And Lion creeps to stroke each precious head.

Bac.: And Wall provides some shelter for a tomb
Wherein the lovers contemplate their doom.

Burb.: And Prologue now becomes the Epitaph
For two young lives dispersed like wind-blown chaff.

(Burbage weeps exaggeratedly. All four look down upon the fallen lovers. There is a pause. Suddenly, Quickly (Thisbe) leaps up, grinning. The lights brighten).

Quick.: I'm Mistress Quickly, not a dead old duck!
So if you thought we'd gone, you're out of luck!

(Quickly helps a grinning Bottome (Pyramus) to his feet. Pyramus links arms with the rest of the cast, in a line behind Quickly, all grinning once more. Bacon is at one end of the line).

Now, masters all, it's nearly time to go.
We hope you've all enjoyed our little show.

So, here's a hat: give cash if you're content.
Then Will and Anne can pay the next month's rent.

(Quickly moves round the audience with the hat, collecting contributions).

Bac.: And I'll put twenty pounds into the pot,
Because I've seen you laughing such a lot.

(Bacon reaches out and puts £20 into the hat, which Quickly then presents to Anne. Anne comes forward).

Anne: We thank you, masters all, for your support.
We hope our play has earned a good report.

(Will comes forward and embraces Anne).

Will: So, Anne and I are surely friends anew.
But to our tale there is a moral too.

Behind each public figure lurks a mate:
They also serve who only stand and wait.

(Will looks adoringly and admiringly at Anne. Anne looks triumphant at last).

End.

B5. Romeo and Juliet.

Cast, in order of appearance.

Nursey:	Juliet's nurse; enjoys everyone's confidence.
Lord Montague:	Head of the Montague family.
Lord Capulet:	Head of the Capulet family.
The Prince:	Overall boss of the city of Verona.
Mercutio:	Related to the Prince; a close friend of Romeo.
Romeo	Son of Lord Montague
Tybalt:	Nephew of Lady Capulet.
Juliet:	Daughter of Lord Capulet
Friar Lawrence:	Friend and confidant of Romeo and Juliet
Crowd,	representing soldiers, citizens, guests, etc.

Tybalt, King of Cats

The play is in five Acts, all taking place in the city of Verona, northern Italy.

Act 1: the Piazza,
Act 2: the masked ball in Lord Capulet's house.
Act 3: the Piazza.
Act 4: Friar Lawrence's cell.
Act 5: a churchyard, in which is the Capulet family crypt.

Act 1: Verona, the piazza.

(Enter Nurse)

Nurse: Now here come I, I'm simply known as Nurse -
A moniker to which I'm not averse.

For, being nameless, people have no cares
In telling me their secret hopes and fears.

So, though Verona's torn by rival factions,
I get to know of future plans and actions.

At present there are two competing hues:
They're called the Capulets and Montagues.

Their rivalry has consequences dire,
As, in our Play, will very soon transpire.

(Enter Lord M with a swagger, followed by Lord C).

Lord M: Now here come I, Lord Montague the Great!
My family are all of high estate.

Lord C: Now here come I, Lord Capulet the Huge!
Don't listen to that jumped-up little stooge!

The Capulets have always been on top.
To Montagues we'll quickly put a stop!

(Lord C draws his sword threateningly)

Lord M: You little squirt! I'll cut you down to size!
For soon you'll feel this sword between your eyes!

(Lord M draws sword and fights Lord C).

Nurse: Help! Help! .... They're at it again. .... H-e-e-l-l-p-p!

(There is a commotion heard offstage. Enter the Prince, with some soldiers).

Prince: Hey! Montague and Capulet! Just cease!
You really must be calm and keep the peace!

I know you're rivals but you surely should
Respect each other, for the common good.

(Lord M & Lord C stop fighting, bow to the Prince & then say ' simultaneously':).

Lord M: Your highness!
Lord C: Your most lofty highness!

Prince: Now, listen both! I hereby do declare:
Henceforth you'll do no fighting anywhere!

Should any blood be spilt, I'll have no pity!
The guilty will be banished from this city.

I'm Prince of all Verona. I'm the Law.
I *won't* abide your squabbling any more.

Shake hands, my Lords, and I'll forget you fought.
Why don't you plan a party? There's a thought!

(The Prince, the soldiers and Lord M & Lord C exit, mumbling to each other about stupid parties. Enter Mercutio).

Mercutio: Now here come I, Mercutio the hearty.
Did I just hear a mention of a party?

Hello, old Nursey! What was all that noise?
Have Monts and Caps again been naughty boys?

Nurse: They had a scrap. But now, to end it all,
Lord Capulet intends to hold a Ball.

He wants his daughter Juliet to marry
A nobleman I think they call Count *Parry.*

Mercutio: Ah, Juliet! Her beauty's all the rage.
But isn't she just 14 years of age?

Nurse: Indeed she is. She also hates Count Parry.
Her dad insists they wed .... event - u - ally.

Mercutio: I have a cunning plan to cheer us all:
I'll don a mask and turn up at the Ball.

I'll bring along my mate, young Romeo.
He's fancied by the ladies, as you know.

He's handsome but he's something of a flirt:
He smiles at anything that wears a skirt.

Nurse: You can't bring Romeo! He's Lord M's son!
No Montague can join the party fun.

Mercutio: Don't worry, Nurse, it is a Ball with Masks.
We're bound to be all right if no one asks.

My cunning plan involves young Juliet.
If Romeo should see her, you can bet

He'll fall in love, and she on him might smile.
She may forget Count Parry for a while.

And, though he's Montague and she is not,
Their friendship might just stop this feuding rot.

Nurse: Mercutio, you are a scheming Gent!
Your plan is bold and is, I'm sure, well meant.

I'll go and say to Lady Juliet:
"Ignore the Count; enjoy the dance; don't fret!"

Mercutio: And I'll away and talk to Romeo,
I'll say that to the masked Ball he must go.

So Romeo and Juliet will meet
And love will glow more brightly in the heat!

(Both exit. End of Act 1).

Act 2. The masked ball in Lord Capulet's house, the next day.

(Enter Mercutio, beckoning to Romeo).

Mercutio: Come, Romeo, and listen to my plan.
Here's sport that will appeal to you, my man!

(Enter Romeo, eager to hear the news).

You like a spot of romance and a dance?
The Cap'let Ball will give you ev'ry chance.

Romeo: Well, here come I: I'm Romeo the beau –
The darling of the ladies, don't you know!

But going to the *Capulet's* masked Ball?
That somehow seems like riding for a fall.

I dreamed last night that I was deep in love,
But with a girl whose love I should not have.

Mercutio: I see Queen Mab has stirred you in your sleep!
She's coaxing you. Be bold, and make the leap

Into the Capulet's domain, to find
The magic girl who's lurking in your mind.

(Romeo & Mercutio put on their masks)

Come! On with masks! Let's go and join the throng.
With all this merriment, thing's *can't* go wrong.

(Enter Lord Capulet, Tybalt, Juliet, Nurse and the other guests at the Masked Ball, though nobody else wears a mask)

Lord C: Now, come into my house and welcome, all!
There's food and drink. Enjoy this special Ball.

Tybalt: I'm Tybalt, and I'm here to see fair play.
I'm making sure no strangers spoil the day.

(Tybalt sees Romeo & Mercutio and draws his sword)

Hey! You two! Let me see your invitation!
I'll throw you out with little hesitation!

Lord C: Relax, young Tybalt! Leave the guests alone.
Tonight let all be welcomed to my home.

(Tybalt lowers his sword & exits, and muttering darkly)

Romeo: Phew! That was close. But who's that lovely girl?
The one who puts my senses in a whirl?

Did my heart love till now? Forswear it, sight!
For I ne'er saw true beauty till this night.

(The other guests gradually exit, leaving Romeo, Juliet and Nurse. Nurse discretely averts her eyes. Romeo and Juliet approach each other. They are entranced and hold hands).

If I profane with my unworthiest hand
This holy shrine, the gentle sin is this –
My lips, two blushing pilgrims, ready stand
To smooth that rough touch with a tender kiss.

(Romeo kisses her hand. Exit Nurse, smiling)

Juliet: Good pilgrim. You do wrong your hand too much,
Which mannerly devotion shows in this;
For saints have hands that pilgrims' hands do touch,
And palm to palm is holy palmers' kiss.

Romeo: Then move not while my prayers' effect I take.
Thus from my lips, by thine, my sin is purg'd.

(They kiss tenderly. Enter Nurse, with a cough)

Nurse: Beg pardon, Miss …. Your mother Lady C
Would like to see you. Can you come with me?

Juliet: Sweet love! I have to take a little walk.
Just wait beneath my window and we'll talk.

(Juliet and Nurse exit)

Romeo: By Jove! The girl I love's a Capulet!
Her name, I do believe, is Juliet!

And I'm a Montague, so there'll be muddle.
She's gorgeous and I love her. That's the trouble.

But, soft! What light through yonder window breaks?
It's Juliet, for whom my heart still aches!

(Juliet appears in an upstairs window)

Juliet: O Romeo, Romeo! Wherefore art thou Romeo?

'Tis but thy name that is my enemy,
For you I'll love for all eternity.

It matters not that you are Montague,
As long as to your Juliet you're true.

Romeo: Oh, I'll be true if thou woul'st marry me!

Juliet: Of course I will. And I'll be true to thee!

Romeo: Let's meet tomorrow at Friar Lawrence Cell.
He'll marry us and all will then be well.

Juliet: Good night, good night! Parting is such sweet sorrow
That I shall say goodnight till it be morrow.

(Exit Romeo and Juliet).

Act 3: The Piazza in Verona, the next day.

(Enter Romeo, Mercutio and Nurse).

Mercutio: Well, Romeo, you dog! Now tell me whether
Fair Juliet and you got on together?

Nurse: It went like wildfire and they're deep in love!
Theirs is a friendship blessed by heav'n above.

Romeo: We're more than friends! At dawn we went to see
The good Friar Lawrence in his cell … and he ….

He *married us*! So we are man and wife!
We've made our vows. We've pledged ourselves for life!

Mercutio: Good grief! What joy! And maybe for a while
The Montagues and Capulets will smile?

(There is shouting outside. Enter Tybalt in a rush. He spots Romeo and draws his sword).

Tybalt: Hey, Romeo! You swine! You should be thrashed!
Last night, unbidden, to our Ball you crashed.

You stinking Montague! You've little right
To be alive at all! Come here and fight!

(Mercutio strides in front of Romeo, to defend him)

Mercutio: Stand back, you King of Cats! Don't squeak and mew!
Ha ha! Look here, I bite my thumb at you!

(Mercutio laughs and makes the classic rude gesture to Tybalt)

Put up your sword. The Prince will have no pity!
If blood is spilt, you're banished from this city!

Tybalt: Away, or draw your sword! You'll have to go!
For naught will stop me fighting Romeo!

(Mercutio, taken by surprise, draws his sword clumsily. Tybalt attacks without delay. They fight. Nurse screams)

You bite your thumb? I'll cut it off! Take that!
I pierce you through for calling me a cat!

(Mercutio falls, dying slowly. Nurse approaches him).

Mercutio: A plague on both your houses! ..... Now you see
Your sword .... has made, has made ... worms' meat of me.

(Mercutio dies. Nurse examines him, then shrieks at the audience).

Nurse: He's dead! He's dead!

Romeo: You've done it now! My oldest friend's no more.
You hot-head! Come, I'll knock you to the floor!

(Romeo draws his sword and fights Tybalt vigorously).

Your feuding is against our city law.
Take that! Now die, and trouble us no more.

(Tybalt is stabbed and quickly falls down dead. The bodies of Mercutio and Tybalt lie together in a heap).

Nurse: Oh, Romeo! He's dead! What have you done?
There's trouble now and so you'd better run!

(Shouting is heard off-stage. Soldiers arrive, followed by Lord Montague, Lord Capulet and the Prince).

Be off before the Prince comes to this place.
It's banishment or death that you will face.

(Romeo rushes out before the soldiers can get him).

Prince: Ho! Soldiers! What's been going on today?
And why these bodies? Who on earth are they?

(The Prince and Lord C examine the bodies lying on the ground).

Lord C: Well, this one's Tybalt. He's a Capulet.
A Montague has done this deed, you bet!

Prince: Well, here's Mercutio, my friend of yore.
I know *he* always tried to keep the law.

Nurse: Indeed he did! For Tybalt came to fight.
Mercutio tried to stop him, as was right.

But Tybalt killed Mercutio and so
Came furiously on to Romeo,

And Romeo fought back in self-defence,
Struck Tybalt dead and therefore fled from hence.

Prince: If what you say is true, it's all a shame.
But Romeo must not return again.

He's banished from Verona. And I say
He shall be killed if he should disobey.

So let this be the end. Let violence cease!
Come, Montagues and Capulets: make peace!

(All except Nurse exit, dragging bodies)

Nurse: Poor Romeo! His banishment's a shame!
He'll never see his Juliet again.

Poor Juliet! Now that her love's departed,
She's all alone. She must be broken hearted.

Lord C will order Juliet to marry
That ghastly nobleman they call Count *Parry.*

I'll go to Juliet and break the news
Of how her Romeo she'll shortly lose.

If anybody knows what should be done
I think perhaps Friar Lawrence is the one.

(Exit Nurse. End of Act 3).

Act 4: At Friar Lawrence's cell.

(Friar Lawrence is seated at his desk, writing. Enter Romeo, looking furtive and dejected).

Lawrence: Hello, poor Romeo, you wand'ring loner.
I hear that you've been banished from Verona.

Fear not, young Sir, your Juliet stays true.
But now she's sadly in a frightful stew.

On Thursday next her Dad will make her marry
That gormless, chinless, wonder called Count Parry.

Romeo: Good grief! She must not wed against her will!
Please tell her that I truly love her still.

To Mantua I'll now in haste repair.
And maybe Juliet can join me there?

Farewell, good Friar, I surely trust in you.
Please write and let me know what we should do.

(Romeo goes out, dejectedly. Friar Lawrence sits at his desk and mutters to the audience)

Lawrence: Good luck to him!. .... I have a cunning plan
For him and Juliet to meet again.

I know of pow'rful drugs that, it is said,
Will make a person seem as if they're dead.

Perhaps, if Juliet could mimic death,
She can deceive whilst still retaining breath.

So if she's left alone for but a day,
Then she to Mantua could steal away.

(Enter Juliet, looking frantic)

Juliet: Oh, Friar! Please help me, for I've quite despaired.
My dearest Romeo has disappeared.

And now my parents say they'll make me marry
That gormless, chinless, idiot Count Parry.

Friar: Your Romeo is safe. He wisely flew
To Mantua, and there he'll wait for you.

I'll write to him and tell him of a way
For you to dodge the Parry wedding day.

So take this drug when you go off to bed.
For two days you will sleep just like the dead.

(Friar hands Juliet a small bottle of magic potion)

Your parents will believe that you've expired.
They'll lay you in the crypt, as we've conspired.

To Romeo I'll say you lie at rest.
He'll come and rescue you, at my behest.

Then both of you can fly without a word,
Before your parents realise what's occurred.

Juliet: This potion seems to me a risky call.
Suppose I wake too soon – or not at all?

(Juliet looks doubtfully at the little bottle)

I'll have to face the music all alone.
I can't tell anyone about this plan.

I'll wake up in a dark and ghostly crypt
Alone, with all my fancy garments stripped.

Friar: Don't worry. Romeo'll be there to hold you.
With strong and loving arms he will enfold you.

I'll write to him and tell him of our plan.
Just put your trust in him, for he's your man!

Now to your bedroom. Say you're feeling sickly.
Then drink the potion. Sleep will come quite quickly.

(Exit Juliet, purposely. Friar mutters to the audience).

Friar: We live in dang'rous times. The plague's about.
And Mantua's in Lockdown, little doubt.

To contact Romeo may soon be fraught.
Our cunning plan risks being set at nought.

(Exit Friar, clutching the letter he's just written to Romeo. End of Act 4).

Act 5: a ghostly churchyard. The Capulet family crypt is to one side, barely visible.

(Enter Romeo with a sword and a small bottle of poison. He's breathless and looks frantically round at the audience).

Romeo: I've come from Mantua. .... Am I too late?
I hear that Juliet has met her fate.

What's happened? There are rumours going round
That Juliet is *dead* and laid to ground!

They say this fam'ly crypt's the very place
Wherein she's laid, a stony slab to grace.

(Romeo points to where the entrance to the crypt can be seen, down to one side).

If true, I've got some poison in this phial,
For life without my Juliet is vile.

I plan to *kill* myself if she has died,
So let me see if Juliet's inside.

Far down into this dreadful crypt I go –
The truth about my love I need to know.

(Romeo crouches and crawls out of sight and into the crypt. Meanwhile, Friar Lawrence and Nurse come onto the stage. Nurse is crying. They do not notice Romeo).

Friar: Come quickly, Nursey. Now's no time for weeping,
For here's the place where Juliet lies sleeping.

Nurse: What do you mean, *asleep*? I'm sure she *died.*
I laid her out myself – gosh, how I cried!

Friar: Ah, no! She took a drug with magic powers
That's made her sleep for eight and forty hours.

She soon should wake and then, without delay,
Her Romeo will take her far away!

Well, that was my intention, as I'd framed it.
And wrote to Romeo and so explained it.

But Mantua's in Lockdown from the plague:
Communication's cut, or very vague.

We *must* find Romeo without delay,
Or else he'll think his Julie's passed away.

Nurse: Let's intercept him, tell him she's asleep,
He's no need to be anxious, nor to weep.

And, by the way, some news: Count Parry's dead:
A balcony collapsed and broke his head!

Though Romeo's no longer got a rival,
We *must* make sure of Romeo's survival.

(Exit Friar Lawrence and Nurse quickly. As soon as they've gone, Romeo emerges on stage. He looks down towards the body of Juliet in the crypt.)

Romeo: Oh, Juliet! My love, you lie so still!
And yet you hardly look as if you're ill.

There's still a touch of crimson in thy cheeks
Where death's pale hand's not stretched to what it seeks.

Though death hath sucked the honey of thy life,
For ever you will be my dearest wife.

So *never* from this palace of dim night
Will I depart again to take my flight.

(Romeo puts the bottle of poison to his lips).

Come, poisoned draught! For ever will I lie
With you, my love. .... Thus, with a kiss, ... I die!

(Romeo falls dead, alongside the body of Juliet. After a pause, Juliet rises slowly and sleepily to come centre stage).

Juliet: How long have I been sleeping? .. Aargh! Who's here?
Whose lifeless body's in the crypt down there?

(Juliet stoops, looks down, then stands up and shrieks in horror)

It's Romeo! My Romeo! .... Now dead?
Let bitter tears caress thy noble head!

(Juliet notices the phial of poison)

What's here? A phial, closed in my true love's hand?
He's taken poison! Now I understand!

(Juliet crouches down weeping, seeming to kiss the corpse of Romeo).

I kiss thy lips: they still feel warm on mine.
Oh! Let me join you in your death sublime!

(Juliet grasps Romeo's sword and stands up)

I take thy sword. ... I plunge it in my heart
That I may die, and thus .... with you .... depart!

(Juliet crumples in a heap, alongside Romeo. At this point, both bodies are in full view of the audience. Enter Nurse and Friar Lawrence. Nurse lets out a scream as she sees the bodies).

Nurse: Good grief! Too late! The pair of them have gone
Together on th' eternal path of doom.

Ho! Call the Watch! .... Let others share this scene!
And mourn two lovers as they might have been:

(The Prince, Lord Montague and Lord Capulet rush in, along with soldiers, attendants, etc.)

Embraced together, in each other's arms
For e'er protected from all earthly harms.

Lord M: }
& Lord C: } Oh no! .... How terrible!
.... What a sight! .... I can't believe it!

Lord M: Friar Lawrence! Please explain this gruesome slaughter!
How come we've lost a precious son and daughter?

Friar: They fell in love at Capulet's masked ball.
I married them soon after, that is all.

Lord M: }
& Lord C: } Married? ....To a Capulet?! ... I don't believe it!
.... To a Montague?! ....Married? I can't believe it!

Lord C: But who? ... But how? .... But why are they now dead?
Who killed them both, and has the killer fled?

Friar: With Rom'eo gone, the way was clear for Parry
To force unwilling Juliet to marry.

But Juliet would never have enjoyed it,
And came to me to help her to avoid it.

I gave to her a drug with magic powers
That made her sleep for eight and forty hours.

The plan was that, as soon as she should waken,
By Romeo she would away be taken.

But things went wrong. He came here whilst she slept.
He thought her dead, and on her body wept.

He took some poison, choosing death's relief.
She woke and found him! Stabbed herself in grief.

Prince: I see each chose togetherness in death:
An everlasting love – but lacking breath.

Here lie two precious payments of the dues
To feuding Capulets and Montagues.

So you, my lords, should bow your heads in shame.
Two lovers dead, and both of you to blame.

(Lords M & C shake hands & remain hugging each other silently. All gather round the corpses).

Let rivalry and envy strictly cease.
Henceforth, let all of us embrace the peace.

For never was a story of more woe
Than this of Juliet and Romeo.

End

C1. A Suffolk Mummers' play.

Cast, in order of appearance.

The Jack	carries a small bell.
King George	carries a sword.
Turkish Knight	carries sword.
Doctor	carries a small medicine bottle.
Big Head	wears a Boar's Head disguise.
Devilly Doubt	carries a broom.

I hope this medicine works quickly!

Mummers

(A bell is heard outside. Enter the Jack, ringing his bell).

Jack: Open the door – and let us in!
The Mummers are coming, your favours to win!

We come in disguises, but nobody fear:
We're clean and we're honest, and full of good cheer.

We've all had our Adnams, or was it Greene King?
And this might account for the mood that we're in.

Now I'm Sproughton Jack; I'm the Enterer-In.
I ask you for space for our play to begin.

So if you'll allow me, I'll call in the crew
And then we'll try bravely to entertain you.

(Enter the rest of the players, who stand in a group).

Now let's have some room! We need gallons of room!
Old Devilly Doubt: he'll be swinging his broom!

DD: Activity young and activity old,
Activity merry, activity bold.

Doc: The company's not of the raggedy sort -
We'll give you good pleasure and plenty of sport.

DD: And if you're well pleased when our playing is through,
Then give us some ale or a mince pie or two.

Jack: For Christmas is truly a time of good will
When poor men like us need some warmth from the chill.

So if you're all ready, let's no more delay.
Step forward King George, - and clear the way!

(King George steps forward to take centre stage)

KG: Now here come I, King George, a knight so bold.
By many a fight I've won my crown of gold.

I rule this land in good Saint Edmund's name,
And with his help I have achieved my fame.

This sword has put a dragon to the slaughter
And saved from death the King of Egypt's daughter.

Show me the man who dares before me stand:
I'll cut him down with one wave of my hand!

(The Turkish Knight steps forward to confront King George).

TK: Now here come I, the Turkish Knight. Bold Slasher is my name.
I've come from Turkish lands afar, and fighting is my game.

I'm here to slash King George to bits, and take his crown of gold.
This trusty sword will stick him through, and make his blood run cold!

KG: Stand off, foul Turkey Snipe, if you be wise,
Or else I'll chop you up as small as flies!

TK: You cannot make me fly an inch! Bold Slasher never flees!
I'll stand my ground, and with this sword I'll cut you down with ease.

My head is made of iron strong, my body's made of steel.
My arms and legs are beaten brass, which you shall shortly feel.

KG: What insolence! I'll make you pay for this!
Pull out thy purse, or else my sword you'll kiss!

TK: Stop up thy mouth! Stick out thy sword! Come, fight,
and don't be shy!
For one of us shall surely live and one of us shall die!

(King George and the Turkish Knight fight).

KG: I'll fight you, Turkey Snipe! You vex me sore.
Stab, Stab! ... I stab you dead! ... So slash no more!

(The Turkish Knight falls down dead).

Jack: Oh horrible Christian! What have you done?
...... You've slain my only son!

KG: I did not start the fight. The Turk began.
Is there a doctor that can cure this man?

Jack: Step forward the doctor!

(The doctor steps forward to view the Turkish Knight's body).

Doc: Now here come I, the doctor true.
Just pay me well and I'll soon cure you!

Jack: Where have you come from?

Doc: Italy, Spitaly, France and Spain;
Round the world and back again!

Jack: What can you cure?

Doc: The sneezes and wheezes, the cramp and the quake,
The dropsy, the poxy, the mulligrub ache;

The flushes and fevers, the high cockalorum,
The drooping and crouping, the sleeping and snorum!

The itch and the stitch, the palsy and gout:
If the devil is in, I'll soon drive him out.

In my little bottle is Elecampane.
One swig of this mixture: you're healthy again!

Jack: What is your fee?

Doc: Ten pounds if you're rich, but five if you're poor.
If you pay me enough, then enough will I cure!

Jack: Then cure this man!

(The doctor pours liquid from his bottle down the Turkish Knight's throat)

Doc: Take a swig of this bottle;
Let it drip down thy throttle.

Rise up, Slasher, and fight again!

(The Turkish Knight gets up. The rest of the cast make way for Big Head).

BH: Now 'ere come I, as ain't been yet,
With my big head and little wit.

Though my head is big and my wit is small,
I can set a song to please you all.

DD: Up come I, Devilly Doubt.
Here's my broom that I swing about.

So if we've pleased you, then give us some cheer
With a pie to eat or a mug of beer.

A bite or a drink when our song is sung,
Or I'll sweep you all to Kingdom Come!

(The company parades round Big Head, Devilly Doubt leading and swinging his broom. They sing a version of the Boar's Head carol (next page). If available, bits of rosemary are strewn round Big Head).

All sing: ♫ The boar's head now you may see
♫ Be-decked with bays and rosemary;
♫ And we pray you, my masters, be merry,
♫ Quot estis in convivio. (1)

♫ Caput apri defero,
♫ Reddens laudes Domino. (2)

♫ The boar's head, as we understand,
♫ Is the bravest dish in all this land,
♫ Which thus bedecked with a gay garland
♫ Let us servire cantico. (3)

♫ Caput apri defero,
♫ Reddens laudes Domino.

(The company parades off, Big Head last, repeating the chorus-line of the song until out of earshot).

End.

Translations:
(1) So many as are at the feast.
(2) I bring the boar's head, giving praises to God.
(3) Serve with a song.

Background notes on the plays.

A1. Olive Cromwell: a restoration comedy.

Although Germaine Greer's book *The Female Eunuch* was published in 1970, I confess that its general message did not get through to me until 1984, when this play was written. This was my first play with gender-reversal, a ploy to which I then returned from time to time.

I have taken liberties in this play when simplifying the history of the English Civil War and the Restoration. It is implied that Prince Rupert Duke of Cumberland, a cavalry commander (or *Cavalier*) acted as the senior Royalist general and that Thomas Fairfax was the leader of the Parliamentary forces (the *Roundheads*) under Oliver Cromwell. But the Civil War itself was rather more complicated. Three phases are usually distinguished: 1642/46, 1648/49 and 1649/51. Charles I was beheaded in 1649. From 1649 to 1653 England was a Commonwealth governed by Parliament. Then Cromwell took personal charge and ruled as Lord Protector from 1653 to his death in 1658. He was nicknamed *Old Ironsides*. Eleanor (Nell) Gwyn was the long-term mistress of Charles II. She lived for a time in a house on Pall Mall, London. The celebrated painter Peter Lely lived from 1618 to 1680.

A2. The Glorious Revolution *or Brother James's Heir.*

This play was written in 1988, when people were recalling the revolutionary events that had taken place 300 years previously. The departure of James II and the arrival of William and Mary were, in truth, attended by a host of complications and minor characters in 1688/89.

James II, who was the son of Charles I and the younger brother of Charles II, came to the throne in 1685. James was born a Protestant but converted to Roman Catholicism in 1670. His two daughters Mary and Ann by his first wife were brought up as Protestants. Mary married her cousin Prince William of Orange, a staunch defender of Protestantism. But then in June 1688, a son and heir (also called James) was born to James II's second wife, an Italian princess. King James was determined to bring up his new and only son and heir as a Catholic. Parliament was aghast at the King's plan. Parliament approached Prince William of Orange as a suitable Protestant candidate to take the throne instead. William assembled an impressive armada and landed unopposed in Torbay in November 1688. In January 1689 Parliament agreed to a joint monarchy, with William as king and James's daughter Mary as queen.

The two new rulers accepted more restrictions from Parliament than had any previous monarch. William and Mary signed the Declaration (or Bill) of Rights which established several constitutional principles, including the right for regular Parliaments, free elections and freedom of speech in Parliament. This Bill of Rights is usually considered to be the first step toward a constitutional monarchy. James II fled to France.

A3. The Great Garter.

This play, written in 1991, was my first to contain explicit Suffolk references. We had moved to Suffolk in 1986 and had become enthusiastic about the county. My play begins in Suffolk, for it was at the Abbey at Bury St. Edmunds that some of the barons met in November 1214 to plan action against the King. The Abbey at Bury itself had reason to dislike King John because he had disregarded the ancient 'Liberty' of Bury by taxing the region and had refused to approve the due election of Hugh as the new Abbot of St. Edmunds. Another Suffolk connection comes through Roger Bigod, Earl of Norfolk and Suffolk, who was a leading light in the Baron's 'revolt'. I have no evidence to connect the legendary East Anglian dog Black Shuk with the Bigods, but the reputedly terrifying nature of Black Shuk seems to fit with the traditional Bigod image. Finally, Queen Isabella of Angoulême appears in my play to emphasise the intertwining of French and English politics at that time. I sometimes think that Isabella's interesting life demands a play in its own right.

A4. The Death of Cardinal Wolsey *or Alas, poor Tom.*

This play sees the end of Ipswich-born Thomas Wolsey and hence the end of his hopes for the County of Suffolk.

Thomas Wolsey was born round about 1471. His father Robert traded as an Ipswich butcher/grazier, amongst other things. By hard work and ruthlessness, Thomas Wolsey rose to the highest secular and ecclesiastical offices in the land and became a Cardinal in 1515. Wolsey's decline began in about 1525, when he had to abandon a plan to raise money by an unpopular tax. His fate was sealed by 1529 with his failure to achieve an annulment of Henry VIII's marriage to Catherine of Aragon.

Wolsey's College at Ipswich was to have been a feeder school for his Oxford foundation (originally named Cardinal College, now called Christ Church), in much the same way as Winchester and New College Oxford are linked. Wolsey's school took its first pupils in 1526 and was granted a Royal Charter in 1528. The project began to evaporate through lack of funds very soon after Wolsey's death. The remaining pupils were re-incorporated into an earlier Ipswich School foundation dating from before 1399. In spite of political upheavals Ipswich School has survived to this day. Two points of detail in the play: the *Pride of Ipswich* was the name of a spritsail sailing barge built in Ipswich in 1864. Joan Lark, whose father was a Thetford innkeeper, was Thomas Wolsey's mistress. She bore him two illegitimate children.

A5. The Hundred Years War, Part One.

This play, which contains echoes of Shakespeare's *Henry V* and the BBC's *Blackadder* series, culminates with the decisive English victory at the Battle of Agincourt. Act 1 takes place in London in 1413. Act 2 takes place in France two years later.

When we first performed the piece in 1997 we painted images of chain-mail-clad soldiers onto a duvet cover, inside of which were several children acting the part of the French army as it repeatedly advanced, collapsed in a heap, re-formed and tried again – a great hoot! We have performed this play several times over the years. I think it is my favourite! On one occasion we got carried away and tried to add the contemporary celebratory song *Deo Gracias Anglia* as background accompaniment but this was a step too far.

The Hundred Year's War between England and France lasted from 1338 to 1453. My play mentions events from the period 1413 to 1420. It starts with the accession of Henry V in 1413, includes the Battle of Agincourt in 1415, and looks forward to the Treaty of Troyes (1420) and Henry's marriage to Catherine of Valois. As for the Battle of Agincourt, the estimated numbers of soldiers and deaths are as follows: English: 6,500 participants, 100 killed; French: 35,500 participants, 9,500 killed.

A6. Richard Coeur de Lion *or Franks Incensed.*

This play describes the adventures of Richard Coeur de Lion during the Third Crusade. I wrote the play in 1998, soon after we acquired a holiday home in Cyprus. We were fascinated by Cypriot history and intrigued to learn that Cyprus had been ruled by the Frankish Lusignan family from 1192 – 1489. The play follows Richard from France in 1190 via Cyprus to the siege of Acre (near modern Haifa) and back via Germany to England in 1194.

A7. Good Queen Bess *or how to survive religion, politics and sex.*
This play follows Queen Elizabeth I from her accession in 1558, via the imprisonment of Mary Queen of Scots in 1567 and Mary's beheading in 1587, the defeat of the Armada in 1588, to the Earl of Essex's traitorous actions in 1598. Elizabeth was a well-educated lady whose principal attributes during these turbulent times were that she remained independent and had a long life. The dates of Drake and Essex have been 'elongated' to suit the plot. Otherwise, historical events happened roughly in the order in which they appear. A contemporary account of Elizabeth's Tilbury speech to "My loving people" includes the following sentence: "I know I have the body of a weak, feeble woman; but I have the heart and stomach of a king, and of a king of England too, and think foul scorn that Parma or Spain, or any prince of Europe, should dare to invade the borders of my realm". It is said that Elizabeth wrote the words herself.

A8. The Belle of Naples *or The Immortal Memory.*
Horatio Nelson was born in 1758, at Burnham Thorpe, Norfolk. He became a midshipman in 1771, aged 13. By the mid-1780s he was commanding a ship on duties in the West Indies. In 1787 Nelson married Frances (Fanny) Nisbet, a young widow from a plantation-owning family on the Island of Nevis. Fanny and Nelson were childless.

Nelson was sent to the Mediterranean in 1793. One of his first duties was to sail to Naples with dispatches for Sir William Hamilton, British Ambassador to the Kingdom of the Two Sicilies. This kingdom embraced all of Italy south of Rome. Nelson's naval career from 1793 to 1805 was a procession of daring encounters, long blockades, brilliant fleet tactics and great personal bravery. On a final note, was Billy Hoste a real midshipman? Yes! William Hoste (1780 – 1828) was a Norfolk lad who went to the same school as Nelson. Extracts from Nelson's letters mention Hoste frequently: "without exception one of the finest boys I ever met with" ... "his gallantry never can be exceeded, and each day rivets him stronger to my heart". Hoste ended an illustrious career as Captain Sir William Hoste, KCB.

A9. Eleanor of Aquitaine.
I wrote this play in the autumn of 2019, when the Brexit debate was coming to some sort of agonised conclusion after the Referendum

result of 2016. The play's first performance was to be at my 80th birthday party in the village Tithe Barn where the audience of over a hundred guests was to include both *Remainers* and *Leavers*. The party was held on 30th November, before the results of the General Election were known. Tricky! Our audience was very familiar with the politicians whose names appear in the play but, for the record, these are: Boris Johnson, Brexit enthusiast and newly-chosen leader of the Conservative Party; Jeremy Corbyn, leader of the Labour Party; Jacob Rees-Mogg, arch-Conservative and enthusiastic Brexiteer; Nicola Sturgeon, leader of the Scottish Nationalist Party; Jo Swinson, leader of the Liberal Democrat party.

Eleanor was born in France in 1122 and died in 1204. She was Duchess of Aquitaine in her own right. She was one of the wealthiest and most powerful women in western Europe of the time. Very well educated, Eleanor was extrovert, lively, intelligent, and strong-willed. Henry Plantagenet, Duke of Normandy, was born in 1133 and died in 1189. In 1154 he became king of England and Eleanor was crowned queen. Henry ruled over England, Normandy, Aquitaine and many other areas of modern France. At various times he also partially controlled Scotland, Wales, the eastern half of Ireland and the Duchy of Brittany – an area that would later come to be called the Angevin Empire.

Eleanor bore Henry five sons and three daughters. During the period from Henry's accession to the birth of Eleanor's youngest son John, affairs in the kingdom were turbulent. By late 1166, Henry's notorious affair with Rosamund Clifford had become known and Eleanor's marriage to Henry appears to have become terminally strained. In March 1173, aggrieved at their lack of power and egged on by Henry's enemies, his sons revolted. Eleanor, who supported them, was imprisoned for the next 16 years. Henry II was followed on the throne by his son Richard and then by John. In our play, Eleanor tries to get Richard and John to think carefully about how they might rule the Angevin Empire when their times come. Are there lessons for our present politicians, I wonder?

A10. The Duke of Bridgewater's Canal.
In Manchester in 1983 our elder son's school project was to research the history of the Bridgewater Canal. As a dutiful parent I got drawn into the project and became enthusiastic. The result was this play. The real events took place between about 1758 and 1765.

The purpose of the canal was to connect the Duke of Bridgewater's coal mines to Manchester. The mines were at Worsley Delf, about 8 miles north-west of Manchester. Transporting coal by canal was much cheaper than the eighteenth-century alternative of horse-drawn carts. The Duke instructed his Agent, John Gilbert, to carry out preliminary surveying of a canal route from Worsley to Manchester. When geographical difficulties were revealed, the Duke contacted James Brindley, an engineer who had established a reputation for mine and other workings involving water. The major engineering challenge in Brindley's new route was the crossing over the River Irwell. This involved building the Barton Aqueduct, which was about 200 yards (180 m) long, 12 yards (11 m) wide and 39 feet (12 m) above the river at its highest point. This aqueduct was thought by many to be impossibly ambitious but was later celebrated as an engineering marvel. The Bridgewater Canal was opened in 1761. It is believed to have been the first canal in Britain to be built without following an existing watercourse. In supplying cheap coal to Manchester, the Duke's canal was important in feeding the energy requirements of a rapidly-expanding industrial centre.

A11. Captain Francis Light *or Far East Suffolk.*
The play takes place in Malaya, between about 1770 and 1794. The first time that I got interested in Penang's story was when I went there as an External Examiner to the University of Science, Malaysia, in 1986-87. On discovering that the 'founder' of Penang was a Suffolk man, I knew I had to investigate further.

Francis Light was born in the village of Dallinghoo, Suffolk, in 1740. After school in Woodbridge and service as a Midshipman in the Navy, Francis joined the East India Company in 1765. He spent the rest of his life in the Company's service overseas, dying on the Island of Penang (Malasia) in 1794. This play is the story of Francis Light's contribution to trade and the British 'colonising' of that part of the world commonly known to Europeans as the *Far East*. Light realised the importance to the East India Company of acquiring a secure harbour somewhere on the sea route between India and China. He gained a reputation as an energetic, just and well-loved administrator. On his tomb in Georgetown, Penang, is this inscription: "In his capacity as Governor, the settlors and natives were greatly attached to him, and by his death had to mourn the loss of one who had watched over their interests as a father". Of course, the implications of such words as 'settlor' and 'native' – and indeed the whole ethos of the East India

Company as a rapacious trading entity – should be set in their historical context. Hindsight is a wonderful thing!

The events described in the play are more or less based on historical fact and real people. Charles, Marquis of Cornwallis (1738 - 1805) came from a family who had owned Brome Hall, near Eye, Suffolk, since the 14th Century. An enlightened Whig politician and intelligent soldier, he was sent to help sort out the rebel Americans in 1776, but was forced to surrender at Yorktown Heights in 1780. He was offered the Governor-Generalship of India in 1782. I have been rather less than fair in portraying the personality of James Scott. In the play he stands as an exemplar for the more outrageous aspect of the British Empire. As for the fictional Chinese servant-girl Mei (meaning 'sister'), she is included as an illustration of how Francis Light seems to have been ahead of his European contemporaries in his attitude to what we might now call human rights. One final point: in the play Scott calls Francis Light a silly Suffolk man, to which Cornwallis, himself a Suffolk man, responds vigorously. Cornwallis is hinting that ‘silly’ should really be the adjective *seely* (Old English *sælig*) which means blessed or holy. With its unusually high number of mediaeval churches, the county has sometimes been called *Seely Suffolk.*

B1. Macbeth.
B2. The Tempest
B3. Omlet.
B5. Romeo and Juliet.

These Shakespeare plays have been simplified from the originals by removing minor characters and reducing scenes that do not materially contribute to the main plots. In some cases, I confess I have removed sections such as Mercutio’s wonderful *Queen Mab* speech (Romeo and Juliet, Act 1 scene 4) with a heavy heart. At the other extreme I could not resist adding a humorous post-script to the carnage at the end of Hamlet. I have added an optional Compère to Macbeth to help younger members of the cast. In all other respects, the central essence of all the Shakespearian plots is retained. I wrote *Romeo and Juliet* in 2020 during the Covid-19 Lockdown. At the time of assembling material for this book’s publication (autumn 2020), my Romeo and Juliet has alas not yet been performed.

B4. Midsummer revels *or Mrs Shakespeare’s Dream.*

Have you ever wondered what Ann Shakespeare really thought of her husband William? Have you also wondered, as you enjoyed *A*

Midsummer Night's Dream, why Shakespeare did not introduce the delightful dramatic efforts of the rude mechanicals into another of his plays? We might imagine that Shakespeare did indeed employ *Pyramus and Thisbe* on another occasion – this time especially for his wife.

The action of this play takes place one evening at The Mermaid Inn, London, in about 1600. There was indeed a Mermaid Tavern in Shakespeare's time and it was a well-known watering place for a group of renowned literary figures including Ben Jonson, John Donne and Francis Beaumont. Although legend has it that Shakespeare also frequented the Mermaid, there is little reliable evidence for this. Furthermore, the Globe Theatre was at Bankside to the south of the River Thames whereas the Mermaid Tavern was a couple of hundred yards north of the river's northern bank. Although sixteen of Shakespeare's plays had been published during his lifetime, these seem to have been mostly without his consent or supervision. At the time of his death, 21 plays remained in manuscript form.

C1. A Suffolk Mummers' play.

Folk plays of this type used to pop up around Christmas time in all parts of mediaeval England. Plays from different parts of the country contain striking similarities. I could not find an example of a specific Suffolk Mummers' play in the literature so decided to write one. Mine is new but is traditional in the sense of incorporating very many words and phrases that have appeared in authentic examples – (see references below). Following tradition, my play has four sections: the presentation; the dispute and fight; the lament and cure; and a seemingly unconnected last phase during which a collection was traditionally made.

References.

1. The English Folk Play, Sir Edmund Chambers, Oxford University Press, 1971.
2. Eight Mummers' Plays, Alex Helm, Ginn & Co. Ltd., 1971.
3. Ipswich through the ages, L J Redstone. Published by East Anglian Magazine Limited, Ipswich. 1948.